EVELYNE LUETHY

OY! PAY ATTENTION!

Verlag: BoD • Books on Demand GmbH, In de Tarpen 42,
22848 Norderstedt
Druck: Libri Plureos GmbH, Friedensallee 273, 22763 Hamburg
ISBN: 978-3-7597-8840-5

Contents

Preface

Personal note from the author

I've always wanted to write a book. I mean who doesn't? It was also obvious to me that it won't be a novel or anything like that. That needs too much planning and keeping track of your characters. I can barely remember my own name.

Up to now, I never felt like I had a story to tell. Then I started writing and I realized that

a) I enjoyed it very much and

b) I had an actual story to tell

Some of the feedback I got on my Substack newsletters also made me seriously consider writing more and collecting it all in a book. This is that book.

How this book works – it's a matrix of topics and steps

The book is organized into four sections, or you could also think of them as steps. There are twelve different topics I deal with in each step. While the book and the chapter numbering follow a step-by-step approach some of you might find it more helpful to read it topic by topic. For that purpose, you find a list of chapters on each topic below.

I'll let everybody explore the different topics on their own, but I do want to say a few words on the different sections. My first step was to **pay attention**. I started noticing things and had a lot of "hang on, what?!" moments. No need to panic, that's what happens when you've been stuck in freeze or survival mode for a long time.

Topic	Time to pay attention	Time to understand	Time to rethink core beliefs	Time to heal
Feelings	I don't want to feel this!	Feelings are real!	Feelings are gifts	You used to be so much happier!
Understanding Trauma	Stuck in the past? - Think again!	Those feelings were hiding where?	You don't have any trauma? What if ...	This is my responsibility? - That sucks!
Harmful Misconceptions	Stop romanticizing resilience!	Resilience does not mean smiling through difficult situations!	It's not a competition!	Linear my ass!
Safe? Safe!	Am I safe?	Feeling safe in today's hate filled world	Shifting the hate within	Feeling safe - with myself
Society sucks!	Victim blaming	An easy way out?	Society taught me what?!	Women? – too complicated!
Stop and think!	Acknowledging feelings	Keeping the peace?	Screw toxic positivity and embrace life	You can't meditate stress away - it's physics!
Who cares?	Do I care?	I'm not alone!	inner child	I'm enough!
Gaslighting	we're in this together	broken finger - suck it up	Advice to younger self	It's everywhere! Calling it out!
Forgiveness	Forgiveness? Nope!	Forgiving myself? Not so fast!	Forgiveness and trauma healing	Consequences and boundaries!
Healing Trauma	Triggers anyone?	The kid brain	You can't analyze trauma away!	A matter of perspective
The Dream	What is my dream?	Is it even possible?	Yes, I can!	I'm a writer
The Journey	thank you kind stranger	I CAN make changes	No quick fixes	Making the scars look pretty – pretty amazing that is

Once you start paying attention you also start **understanding** patterns. You see why some societal norms are harmful. You realize just how stuck you are – it's a sobering stage. And it's followed by an even tougher step. That's where you start **rethinking core beliefs**. It's where you realize that your entire life has been a big old lie, where it all starts crumbling down and you're having to rebuild it almost from scratch.

Finally, it's time to **heal** – a very non-linear step. Also, like the others, not one that's ever finished. I mean, what does "healing" even mean in this context?

I don't claim to have all the answers. Far from it. What I do know is where I was and where I am now and that it's been an insane journey. I'm still very much a work in progress but I've come extremely far those past four years and that's why I'm writing this book. To give others maybe just an impulse of what to look for and where to start (it doesn't really matter where, everything will fall into place eventually). And to give hope.

Topics & chapters

If you're interested in reading about specific topics in order, here's a little overview of where you can find the respective chapters. Basically, just add twelve to get to the next one.

Disclaimers

First: This book is based entirely on my own experience.

While I do hold a bachelor's degree in psychology, I'm not a mental health professional – at all. I'm sharing my experience based on - my experience. I don't claim to have any data backing up what I write. So, I won't be quoting studies or listing sources. This is my own work. I will give credit where I remember how I got to examine a certain topic more closely. This is the exception though. The entire process was very much my own and felt like a natural progression. Sometimes a key word is all that's needed for things to start making sense – if you let it.

Second: Seek professional help when struggling.

Please seek professional help if you're struggling. While I might be able to point you in the right direction or help you figure out how to find answers for yourself, a licensed (trauma) therapist can do so much more. Either way, why not talk to people about your mental health – good or bad. You got this!

Introduction

Ever wondered why there are so many self-help books in even the smallest bookshop? Well, there are millions of situations, sensations or experiences each day that have the capacity of screwing with our mind. Now let's assume that one in a million might do just that. Multiply that by the number of days you've been alive, allowing for similar experiences to accumulate over time, and you end up pretty messed up. With me so far?

This might be your first "yet, but!" moment reading this book and there'll be many more. That's a promise. Do me a favor and just assume that I'm right for a minute and see what that does to you. I talk a lot about triggers and about acknowledging how certain situations, statements etc. make us feel. This is your chance to experience it firsthand.

If you then still think that I'm 100 % wrong – get in touch and I'll explain why I'm right.

Already triggered by that? It's gonna be a long freaking book for you to get through then. That was what we commonly refer to as a *drumroll* - joke. There might be some scattered throughout because while I do write about mental health and difficult feelings, I also like to have a bit of a laugh once in a while. I'm even funnier in Swiss German, but only a fraction of you will ever see proof of that. It's a secret language.

Typos? Grammar or spelling mistake? Sure, those shouldn't happen. Of course they shouldn't. But they clearly do. I knew I should have written this book in Swiss German – 20/20 hindsight. That's a language with no spelling rules whatsoever. It just would have made things so much easier - for me.

But I digress – also something you can expect from this book.

You will find inconsistencies because some topics are not black and white and looking at them from different angles give you slightly different insights. If you found some and they bother you, please go back and find more. There's always more.

And then get in touch and – well, you get the picture.

You're in for an interesting ride. Best buckle up. This book will make you angry at times, sad at others, hopefully also laugh out loud and give you hope. It's my journey from the brink of suicide to where I am now – actually enjoying my life. I almost said thriving but managed to stop myself in time.

I'm not in psychotherapy because something is wrong with me. I'm in therapy because my body and mind reacted and are still reacting perfectly to some seriously messed up crap that happened in my childhood.

So … I've been asking myself.

How is that my fault? How am I the one who is stigmatized? I call bs!

And that's WHERE your journey begins.

STEP I: TIME TO PAY ATTENTION

1 I don't want to feel this!

FEELINGS – TIME TO PAY ATTENTION

Let me start by saying that feelings are scary. Super scary. They just appear out of nowhere and you have no control over when, where or how. None whatsoever! And don't get me started on mindfulness and such. Yes, we are jumping in at the deep end – grab your floaties and off we go.

Of course, you can let emotions and thoughts float by and not deal with them right away. You can't control them appearing though; nor should that be your goal. It's like not eating for a few days; it can be helpful, but doesn't usually solve your everyday problems with eating, overeating or bingeing. Same with thoughts and feelings. Best to learn how to cope in everyday situations.

Emotions can be triggered by a smell, a sound, a song on the radio, a face, a voice or just a thought, a memory. Unless you're a robot you can't avoid emotions. What you can do is learn how to acknowledge them and work with them – not against them.

Imagine you yourself are an emotion and you want to and need to be heard. Your human is constantly ignoring you and pushing you away. And you're not the only one. There's an entire group of you. You get bored and angry – even if you are not "anger". You look for other places to go. How about if I pinch here or cut through this. Emotions get up to all sorts of stuff if they are ignored.

Ever have random sharp pain? There you go. Best not to mess with them.

A lot of us women have been told from a young age not to be angry, not to lash out, not to show any negative emotions. Same for men with emotions commonly associated with weakness, I guess. I can only really speak from the *girl that was told not to get angry* perspective. Yes, girls are just supposed to smile pretty and not be loud – ever.

Oh, the toxicity. Don't worry, we'll get into that.

It has changed some but there is a lot of work still to do. For everybody really. Girls are allowed to cry and get emotional, but never angry. Boys are allowed to get angry and punch people, but never cry. This shit goes deep. And as I said above, those feelings don't just go away. They are stuck in your body until you're willing, able or allowed to feel them.

For some of you they might run out of space inside your body. Additions need to be built. Hello extra body weight. Over simplified and not based on science – I know. I'm basing this solely on my own experience with emotions and the same ones reappearing whenever I was losing weight only for me to panic, and pile on yet more weight, because I didn't want to feel that emotion.

Sound familiar?

2 Stuck in the past? – Think again!

UNDERSTANDING TRAUMA – TIME TO PAY ATTENTION

I don't know how this chapter happened. Somehow my brain paid attention to things happening around me and I just started typing and emotions and tears started flowing. It all began with traditions and how people like them. Right now, carnivals are going on all over the place. Personally, I'm glad that's not really a thing where I live but that's just me.

This led me to why people like traditions. I mean, objectively, to still do what somebody hundreds or even thousands of years ago thought was a good idea, is a bit weird. Especially when embracing change or progress elsewhere. Are we off the hook because there's comfort in traditions? After all there's comfort in repetition. There's comfort in what we know and are used to. There's comfort in familiarity.

Yet, we're telling people who have childhood trauma to just move on. To not be stuck in the past. We're telling people to let go of everything that is familiar to them. Of everything they know.

Re-learning your entire life is not done by just moving on. A lot of the time there is no frame of reference of what is "normal", of what is healthy. And a lot of the time it's the people who are telling us to move on that are very much stuck in the past themselves. Of course, in their case it's church or state sanctioned stuckness – it's religious or tradition. And that's obviously different, right?

If you've grown up in a toxic environment, you need to very literally re-learn how to live. You need to question EVERYTHING you ever believed, about life, about family, about friendship, about yourself. Do you realize how difficult that is? Letting go of everything you thought you knew about life. Letting go of everything that is familiar to you? Realizing that people who feel safe might be the opposite. Try navigating that. It's very much a game of getting up and being knocked down over and over again.

When you grow up like that you don't trust your feelings. Your feelings have never matched your lived experience. You were forced to stop trusting them. You were forced to stop doing what you knew was right. Who you were forced to become is nowhere close to who you truly are. Untangle that!

Yes, you can get help letting go of the pain, but that doesn't teach you how to live without it.

Yes, you can work through the trauma and get out of survival mode, but survival mode was your safety blanket. How do you live without that?

Yes, you can let go of what's been weighing you down, but how do you stand tall? This was your suit of armor.

I don't have all those answers yet, I'm a work in progress. But I can raise awareness of what it's like to have a lot of adverse childhood experiences and what it takes to break free.

3 Stop Romanticizing Resilience!

HARMFUL MISCONCEPTIONS – TIME TO PAY ATTENTION

When you wake up at 5 AM on your day off and it's still dark because it's winter, you kinda have to scroll through Instagram. I think that's the rule. It was a bit early to pay attention, but a reel caught mine. I might not have used those exact words myself, it's close enough for me to quote part of what was said. Several people have used this, so I don't know who to give credit to.

> ➤ I don't find it flattering when you call me resilient.
> ➤ I'm so exhausted by my strength.
> ➤ I'm tired of people romanticizing my urgency and ambition as if I had any other choice.

Trauma doesn't make you stronger – it traumatizes you. PERIOD. That's it. End of story.

Well, not quite... I used to buy into the whole *what doesn't kill you makes you stronger* mentality. I might have even said that in a newsletter. Then I realized the harmful message behind it.

It takes a lot of strength and effort to get up again, to embark on the healing journey. And I made a promise to myself that I wasn't going to sugarcoat the hours and days of lying on the floor in a crying heap until there were no tears left.

And that's exactly why I won't shut up about it. Especially when I see how people are traumatized left, right and center. War is an obvious one. How we seem to have entered a competition of who can do the most atrocious things to fellow human beings, of who can inflict the most pain in the name of whatever or whoever is beyond comprehension.

Then there's abuse cases that are made public the scales of which are incomprehensible. There's no knowing how much abuse happens behind closed doors at the hands of family. You know, people you should feel safe with. At home where you're "safe".

And don't think small children can't be traumatized because they are too young to remember. The body remembers. My first big T Trauma happened

8

in the womb. Took me a while to figure out, but the body remembers. Your nervous system remembers.

There is so much pain and suffering out there. So many lives forever scarred. So many childhoods lost. So many nightmares lived. "Time heals all wounds" just popped into my head. It doesn't. It really doesn't. We can't sit and wait for the wounds to be healed. Some wounds will never fully heal. Just like visible physical scars. They healed as much as they could. And sometimes they still hurt.

Children should feel safe growing up. Children should not have to worry about clean water, food or bare necessities. Children should not be woken up by sirens. Children should not see their friends die. Children should not live in fear. And home should be a safe place – always.

Resilience isn't something to praise people for. We didn't have a choice. And can we please stop saying *what doesn't kill you makes you stronger*? It's a weird way of romanticizing not only resilience but also the harmful situation/action that traumatized us.

Thank you.

4 Safe?

I am lucky to live in a reasonably safe country. And on a day-to-day basis I'd say that I feel safe. Yes, there might be the odd time when I'm alone somewhere at night and I'm a bit more vigilant. Of course there is. But living in Switzerland I never gave feeling safe much thought before I started my healing process.

At some point I came across the term "survival mode". I can't remember where I heard it first but it kind of seemed to fit my situation. And when I started paying attention, I realized that I was always – and I mean ALWAYS – on high alert. My body was unable to relax. I mean even after a nice massage or a sauna, it was impossible for my body to truly relax.

This was my normal though and at that point I didn't realize how much work I would have to do to get out of survival mode. My fight or flight response was just on all the time.

I was feeling overwhelmed. My body was stressed. I woke up at 3 AM every morning, which I read can be due to high cortisol levels. I was emotionally all over the place. People pleasing was also something that fed into the entire situation – always putting my needs last. Making sure everybody was okay before I thought about what I wanted or needed.

What I just wrote in a paragraph took me several months to realize. And of course that was only the beginning. Total tip of the iceberg. I needed to go back to moments where I didn't feel safe to start healing.

It was around that time that I read a crime novel where the protagonist was having night terrors. For some reason I could really relate to that. And somehow it made me realize that I was safe. I was living in an apartment all by myself. There was no reason to feel stressed, there was no longer a reason to jump at every noise or to listen for footsteps.

That realization didn't really help all that much at first. My body was not letting anything go. It was convinced I was still in danger, and it was determined to keep me safe. I needed to find a gentle approach to convince my body that I was - in fact - safe.

Next, sleeping through the night became a bit of a problem. I felt even more overwhelmed now that I was paying attention. It was almost impossible to get out of this freeze state and actually do things I wanted to do. I could literally sit there and think "I would love to go for a bike ride now", and physically be unable to get up and go.

Yes that could also be ADHD paralysis, but in this case it wasn't.

Apparently, your brain and specifically your prefrontal cortex knowing you're safe and your body (including your amygdala – where the fight/flight response lives in the brain) feeling safe and happy are two entirely different ball games. They might not even both be played with balls.

Why is this so complicated?

5 Victim blaming

SOCIETY SUCKS! TIME TO PAY ATTENTION

I've been working on overcoming childhood trauma for years. One of the biggest lessons I learned was that I am not to blame for what happened to me. Sounds simple, doesn't it? Well, it isn't. Victim blaming is so ingrained in us that it's difficult to change that mindset. "Oh, you got beat up a lot when you were young – well, you must have misbehaved". This is so messed up! And it lets the perpetrator off the hook.

Once you realize this and start paying attention, you find it all over the place.

There are religious groups who take victim blaming to the next level. If anything happens to one of the girls, it is their fault, because they either had lustful thoughts or were wearing something to defraud [that's fundie speak for "seduce"] a boy/man.

A lot of women grow up thinking that a man's behavior towards them is their responsibility – no matter what the situation. Parents are told to protect their daughters. How about parents educate their sons AND daughters?

As long as we put the responsibility solely on the girls and women, things are not going to change. That should be obvious to everybody. Victim blaming by society leaves people not only traumatized from the assault itself but also retraumatized because nobody believes them or they even get blamed. If that is your experience the reaction of your environment can leave a much deeper wound than the assault itself.

Newsflash to the *she had it coming wearing that* crowd: you can wear the baggiest clothes, no make-up, hair in a messy bun and this can still be seen as an invitation to be cat called, hit on, touched inappropriately etc.

Off the top of my head, I can think of five instances of unwanted physical contact in my adult life (I'm sure there's more, but we're trained to just brush those off) and here's what I was wearing at the time: very loose-fitting winter outfit (2x), a firefighting uniform, jeans and a baggy t-shirt

(2x). None of these instances were at parties, involved me drinking (I don't drink) nor did I have any previous contact with the men involved. So don't go telling me that this only happens to drunk women, who dress "inappropriately" at parties and lead men on.

Pay attention! Listen to what women are telling you.

I can now hold my own and in a recent case shouted "leave me the fuck alone" at a guy following me around a Dutch city, trying to grab my arm, insisting I HAD TO go have coffee with him just because he happened to see me walking down the street, proved very effective. People were ready to jump in and he got the message.

However, we're not always in a situation where we can speak up, where we can put up a fight, where we are even old enough to know that what's happening is not okay, where it is safe to do so, where we are believed.

None of that is our fault.

Society needs to do better! Society needs to pay attention!

6 Acknowledging feelings

STOP AND THINK! – TIME TO PAY ATTENTION

One of the biggest lessons I learned during my trauma healing process was that every feeling is there for a reason. And that this very feeling needs to be acknowledged. It can be as simple as "I'm feeling really sad right now – I wonder why" and then moving on with your day. That sense of wonder is all that's needed for your mind and body to know it's okay to feel e.g. sad or angry. Maybe you'll find out later what triggered that feeling, maybe you won't. The important message is that every feeling is okay. Every feeling is a message. Forcing yourself to stop feeling sad or angry, because … "happy" – that's just wrong.

It doesn't take much time and effort to pay attention. It takes a bit of practice. Notice a feeling, acknowledge it with a sense of wonderment. That's it.

I grew up thinking that happy was the desired state. So, I pretended to be happy. You know how much effort that takes? And how bad you feel because you don't feel happy all the time? Your expectation that you need to feel happy makes you ignore negative feelings by just pretending everything is okay. Your glass might look half full, and the water might look clean, but it's like somebody pooped in it. You can't keep drinking it. It'll make you sick. And no, I'm not apologizing for that mental image.

OMD! I just had a Barbie (the movie) flashback. I think that's what bothered me about it. The toxic positivity portrayed at the beginning. It was just way too happy (and pink and plastic) and the expectation was for everybody to be happy. That was the default setting. How utterly boring and toxic.

What is happiness to me? What makes me happy? That I can feel all these wonderful and not so wonderful emotions without guilt, shame and trying to avoid them. They are what make us human. They are like friends who show up once in a while to highlight what is happening and to draw your attention to certain situations.

And just like other friends, sometimes you can tell them that you appreciate their input, but that you don't have the capacity to process what they're telling you right now. That's a way of managing your emotions. You acknowledge them and then you can shift your focus to something happier, to something positive. You don't have to dwell on negative emotions every time you have them. Come back to them when you can. It's suppressing emotions or pretending they are not there that is harmful and very much so.

It's the difference between "I don't want to feel angry" and "I feel angry – I guess that's understandable given the situation". The latter thought will help us move on; the former will make us feel stuck in the long run.

7 Do I care?

So here I was wondering if anybody even cares how I'm doing. Sure didn't seem like it. People who asked me how I was doing, didn't really want to get a real answer. Also, what was I expecting everybody to do anyway? Nobody was coming to save me. I was stuck in this pattern of helplessness from way back when. I hadn't realized that I was responsible for taking care of this myself.

The problem was, I was not ready for that. And my life was all about what other people wanted or needed. I was programmed to put everybody else's needs above mine.

Yet here I was craving attention. Yet here I was feeling short-changed. Yet here I was waiting for somebody to care. Waiting for somebody to make me matter. Waiting for somebody to make up for all those needs that weren't met when I was little.

I know this now. I didn't know that then. I had no idea that that's what I was doing. None whatsoever. I even read somewhere that people with childhood trauma of unmet needs were waiting for somebody to save them and that the healing starts when you realize this is meant to be you yourself. I was like "okay", and continued living the exact opposite way.

That might have looked something like "I don't want to speak up and say what I need but I will just eat an extra piece of cake at their place to make up for it". All that bargaining – because they didn't give me something (something I never even asked for of course), so I will get something else back by doing this.

I wasn't thinking that out loud. I wasn't even thinking this quietly. I didn't know this was what I was doing. Not communicating my needs, not asking for help. Does hyper independence ring any bells?

Writing this book and starting to pay attention to my own behavioral patterns – starting to; there's so much more to come, I realized that I didn't really care for myself. I never learned how to care for ME. That's something that is usually modeled for you as a child. You watch how people in your environment care for themselves. Trouble is - if they don't, how are you going to learn?

A pattern I noticed was to say "I don't care" or "it doesn't matter" when somebody asked me what I wanted to do, eat etc. Now here comes the problem. Every time I didn't speak up, my self-worth shrank a little bit. I mean, of course there has to be room for compromise, but the other person needs to know you are compromising. If you only do it in your head while quietly grumbling – that's not going to work, is it?

You know how difficult this is after almost 50 decades on this planet? I've only just realized how all this fits together and let me tell you, I'm still coming to grips with it. But what I can firmly say now – I care. And I'm going to get this trainwreck back on track. That's a promise to myself.

8 We're in this together

GASLIGHTING – TIME TO PAY ATTENTION

The realization that we're all in this together was a big one. There is a need for systemic change. There is a need to start listening. Whether it be "Black Lives Matter" or "marriage for all" or women's (reproductive) rights.

When I started paying attention to gaslighting I realized that societal gaslighting had been happening my entire life. We're told to feel good about ourselves and that we are okay just the way we are, right? Nice enough message, but why did I start seeing ads on how to improve myself on TV as a kindergartener and whenever I went to a store as a teenager?

Nowadays it's Instagram etc. I'm constantly bombarded with make-up tips, because apparently my face needs improving. I own no make-up, nor have I ever clicked or lingered on anything related to make-up. I also get a lot of *how to find the right man* ads – seriously algorithms take a hint!

When I spoke up in a newsletter about victim blaming and having been harassed and sexually assaulted by men on several occasions, I got the old "not all men" response followed by "this happens to men too". Missing the point entirely and this is MY story.

There are many systemic problems in this world and here's how I would like us to tackle them instead:

- ➢ don't try and silence a person's voice because their story triggers you (if it does, might you be part of the problem)

- ➢ acknowledge that there is a systemic problem even if you feel like you're not a part of it (not all men and such)

- ➢ listen to people's stories without gaslighting them into thinking it's all not true or not that bad (I was guilty of that regarding racism – then I started listening to the people affected and those in the Black Lives Matter movement; I'm still a work in progress)

> call out the behavior in question when you see it – not always possible, I know; sadly, there are enough instances where it is possible

And this is where I realized that tackling any systemic problem helps everybody and that we are in this together.

Let me give you an example. Let's say I'm targeted by weight loss ads. As an eating disorder survivor this can be particularly harmful. In this case I'm speaking up about societal beauty standards and raising awareness about how harmful they can be. For the longest time I saw those ads and didn't see them as gaslighting, but they are essentially telling people that they can't possibly like their bodies, faces, hair etc. if they don't look like the heavily photoshopped person in their ad. At the same time society is telling us to love ourselves. A very toxic combination and impossible to live up to.

Yes, eating disorders affect more women than men. Hell, we get targeted by all those ads from a very young age (pre-social media it was on TV and in magazines) – correlation anyone? But tackling the root of those problems will help everybody. And that's what it means to tackle systemic problems. Everybody wins.

We all have experiences that shape us. I speak to the ones that affect me or have affected me growing up. And you know what – societal gaslighting sucks!

9 Forgiveness? Nope!

Along with people saying that you need to move on and not be stuck in the past, they will tell you to forgive any perpetrators because not doing so is holding you back. And they truly believe this to be the case.

When I started paying attention to my feelings and to what I wanted to do about things, I realized that forgiveness felt like I was letting myself down and it took me forever to figure out why this felt wrong. It felt like I was telling the person that I was okay with how they treated me – and I was most definitely not okay with that.

What I also started realizing was that forgiveness had this strong link to religion for me. I think it's this passage in the Lord's Prayer "and forgive us our trespasses, as we forgive those who trespass against us" and all that talk about turning the other cheek, loving your enemies and such.

Very unhelpful.

This also reminded me of abuse scandals and how those perpetrators sought forgiveness, received it because the victims were forced into it and then just kept doing the same thing over and over again.

I felt very underwhelmed when I realized that forgiveness clearly didn't work. The entire time I was making excuses for people and defending or downplaying their actions when some of them didn't even seek forgiveness. Nor was there ever any change in behavior on the horizon. There's even less of a point in forgiving someone who doesn't even acknowledge that they did something to hurt you. Forgiving someone who didn't even apologize to you. Or who is adamant they didn't do it.

This was not what I wanted at all. This was not what I needed. This was infuriating. This was re-traumatizing. And I really felt for other survivors. I started thinking about if anything even changes for them or us when people pretend to repent, seek forgiveness and we forgive them. It's like they are acknowledging what we already know – that they did something wrong.

Once you realize what always being the bigger person, always putting yourself last, being told that they couldn't help it, does to you - there's no going back.

Where are the consequences if we have to forgive everything? There aren't any. The behavior just keeps happening over and over again. There are so many examples of this. Them asking for forgiveness without changing their behavior in any way is not a way of helping survivors heal.

And then there is this fraction of people who think that an abuse survivor played an active part in the abuse. The victim blaming and the cover up is one of the worst things that could happen to a survivor. It's also why a lot of us are lured into forgiveness. We're forced to forgive because it's really not their fault. We are to blame just as much. It could even go as far as us having to apologize and seek forgiveness for the abuse we suffered. How messed up this is becomes clear when we think of abuse that happens in early childhood. It's just bizarre.

That forgiveness doesn't work became glaringly obvious to me, but what did I do with that newfound insight?

10 Triggers anyone?

HEALING TRAUMA – TIME TO PAY ATTENTION

Sure – we all have them, but what are they and why are they useful?

Triggers tell us something about ourselves, possibly pointing us to a past experience that could use some reprocessing. Or they remind us of how we lived. Our lived experience is what informs our triggers.

We all tend to take things personally and get offended by stuff that has nothing to do with us. This is used for clicks, likes and comments on social media. People are making claims they know are false and are counting on others to tell them as much. Put an embarrassing typo in a post and you'll get more replies on that then on the actual message. I used to fall for this and correct people. I used to be a teacher. That's my excuse.

Some people get attacked for what they are saying as if they said it to every single person on social media individually. They don't know who reads it, so how could they have meant you? I've started to **not** react when I get triggered by something somebody said. That's incredibly difficult. But even just paying attention to it and trying was an interesting experiment.

And it was difficult to realize that any adult person is responsible for their own triggers. You can't blame others for triggering you. Unless it's deliberate and hurtful, but that's not what I'm talking about. I mean getting triggered by something you read, hear, see, smell or touch. The kind of trigger that's a chance for you to grow or heal.

There are a few things I started doing and that have helped me use triggers to my advantage. In a first step I just noticed them. I paid attention to my reaction. That's all I did. Then I started writing down when or how I got triggered. Just putting a bit more focus on that situation. Is there a pattern? Are there certain emotions that get triggered? I acknowledged those. Entirely without judgement. I looked at them like somebody I hadn't seen in years and welcomed them.

Do I like all the feelings that get triggered?

Well, of course not. Some of them are really difficult. I take my time to go with those feelings and look deeper. This is the one step you can't force. If the feeling is too intense at that moment with the spotlight on it, that's perfectly okay. Notice it, acknowledge it's too intense and know you can come back to it some other time.

Depending on how deep the wound that needs healing is, this might take many attempts. Be patient and gentle with yourself here. This also needs a safe space and quite a bit of practice. Trauma healing is a marathon – not a sprint. Go at your own pace. And remember not to let a therapist rush you either.

One more thing: What caused that feeling in the first place – way back when, is not important. It might be interesting – yes; but it's not necessary to know in order to heal.

Just pay attention.

11 What is my dream?

I'm sure you've had people ask you "What do you want to do when you grow up?" or "If you could do anything, what would you do?". What were your answers? Did you really explore EVERYTHING? Or did you limit your thoughts to what is reasonable, doable and what wouldn't make people laugh? Take a minute to think about this.

Now, what happens if we change that question to "what is your dream?". My mind immediately shifts to everything that I could possibly ever want to do. It doesn't have to be realistic, reasonable, or even possible. The sky's the limit. When a friend asked me that question 2.5 years ago, I felt my mind opening and I said something I hadn't realized was my dream. Okay, it also took me forever to even come up with an answer and I then just hesitantly went with the first thing that had popped up.

It was something I had never told anybody. It was something that came from deep inside and that I wasn't aware of. From that day onward it was there, and it was there to stay. I'm not sure if I need to follow it fully, but I have certainly started following a path to creativity. Writing was part of that dream. And writing gives me so much energy it's insane. More than I ever thought possible or expected. I guess this is what it feels like when you do what you truly love.

I never questioned how I could write a 5-page essay in a couple of hours back at university when it took my classmates days, nor did I ever really think about it. It was just something I could do, and others couldn't. We all have things like that.

It's easier to dream with supportive friends in your life. Society is crushing all our dreams at an early age. How many times have you heard or even said "yes, but can you make money doing that?". Or, and this is one of my favorites, "okay, but you need to learn a trade first". This was in Switzerland where apprenticeships are the norm, and kids are entering the workforce at around 16.

So, let's all postpone our happiness because society is not made for people living their dreams! I'm not going to go into a rant here, don't worry. I understand why parents would say that. I really do. I just wish there was more of a *let's see how we can help you work towards your dream while getting the education we feel you need* kind of mindset out there. I don't like to see teenagers' dreams being squashed the way they are. Or anybody's dreams for that matter.

Back to you! Just imagine how amazing it would feel if you did something that made you truly happy and how much energy that would give you. Stay with that feeling for a moment.

Isn't it wonderful? Go out there and dream. Dream like you've never dreamed before. AND DREAM BIG!

12 Thank you – kind stranger!

Some of you already know this story but I've decided to share it here too. Sort of as a starting point to me turning my life around and getting to where I am now. It all started with a social media message from a follower.

I didn't share much on social media, in real life or anywhere. Nobody knew what was really going on. That didn't stop them from sending me a message of encouragement. Was I receptive to this message? Well, not initially. It made me angry. I was like "well what do you know? It is not that easy! Do you even know what you're talking about?". Of course, I didn't say all that, I only thought it. Still this message had two effects.

First, it made me angry and that stopped me in my tracks. I was ready to just end it all. Not going to say more about that. It was a very dark time. Whoever's been there doesn't need me to explain and whoever hasn't, be glad you don't know and hope you never find out.

Secondly, it planted a seed of possibility. Were they right? Was change really possible? Could I really do it? Me? The person who had failed so many times before.

There I was at a very low point and this person on social media had the audacity of making anything sound possible. How dare they do that?! They knew nothing about me. I barely even shared my name back then.

Yet, that seed of possibility was firmly planted.

Of course, this had to happen at the beginning of 2020, so instead of moving on quite quickly I was stuck in a bad situation for another eight months. And I knew that despite deciding to make very necessary changes in my life, I still had a lot of work to do and a lot of challenges to face.

In my case a complete change of environment was needed. I finally managed to move out in October of 2020. And almost immediately I made brand-new friends online. The encouraging and compassionate kind. The year had been tough on everybody – I mean what a shit show that was. I was so happy to have people basically carry me through this tough period of my life.

Four years on I feel stronger than ever. I still have some healing to do but I've come a long way.

It all started with that one encouraging message.

Remember to be kind, you never know what people are going through.

This is a real-life example. Thank you – friend!

Wherever you are, whatever you are going through, please know that you are not alone, you are enough, and you can totally do this!

STEP II: TIME TO UNDERSTAND

13 Feelings are real!

FEELINGS – TIME TO UNDERSTAND

This is me starting to believe that feelings are okay. I needed a lot of help understanding this. A lot of help. I had never given feelings much thought. I had them. Period. The ones I didn't want I pushed away or down with a block of chocolate. I didn't even attempt to actually feel them. I don't want to feel angry – chocolate (or other food); I don't want to feel sad – food again; I'm scared of feeling happy – food once more. You get the picture.

What started the ball rolling was a message from a friend who'd written a song in which he said, "feelings are not a fact but they are real". It was a long message explaining what he meant by that. It took me a while to get on board with it and once I did, things started changing.

I tried to just acknowledge any feeling I had. That was all I did initially.

This took a lot of practice. So much practice! I was quickly trying to get rid of so-called bad feelings. Then I realized that feeling angry didn't make me a bad person and that I didn't have to act on it either. It's one thing to feel angry and express this to yourself or to somebody else. That doesn't mean you have to beat them up.

Also, you might feel like a failure for not completing a goal you had set. Huge disappointment. Does that actually make you a failure? Nope.

Feelings are not a fact, but they are there for a reason. What a game changer. And something to remember.

I had never learned how to feel and how to regulate my emotions – positive or negative ones. So, here's what I do now that I've started to understand how they work. I acknowledge them, feel them (if appropriate at the time) and decide if they are useful to me at that very moment. Then I either deal with them right then and there or I let them be. I can always come back to them.

Dealing with emotions can take on different forms. It can be sitting with a feeling to figure out why it's there. It can be shifting the focus away from it, changing the perspective. There are many different ways and I will be exploring some of them throughout the book. My message to you right now is to start acknowledging the feelings you have. In a further step you're gonna find your own way of regulating them if you need to. I can only share what worked/works for me.

I keep going back to what I was told about feelings being real. Sometimes I'm still having a difficult time accepting that. It's when feelings pop up that I'm ashamed of. In such cases admitting that I feel that way is extremely hard to accept. Yet, acceptance is the key to moving forward.

Why are feelings so complicated? Or are they?

14 Those feelings were hiding where?

Time to understand what your kid brain is doing. I'm gonna start with an example. It was an unexpected one for me. My sister died when I was five. I never grieved for her – partly because I was blaming myself, partly because I didn't know how. And as the situation was at the time nobody taught me how to grieve either. That's how it turned into complicated grief for which I did seek professional help a couple of decades ago. After that period where I was in therapy memories kept popping up now and then, but I didn't think much of it. Nor did we ever get to the bottom of anything.

As a way of honoring my sister I started lighting a candle on her birthday and another one on the day she died. Just a few moments of reflection. During a recent therapy session (specific trauma therapy using EMDR), I found out why those memories had kept popping up as they did over the years. We looked at what memories I had relating to my sister. And what do you know. I found one that carried so much more weight than her actual death. I was blown away by that.

Don't get me wrong. Of course, I realize that it's very seldom only one single traumatic event that leaves us wounded. Other things are going on at the same time and can be linked. It usually feels like peeling an onion and uncovering more and more related memories. That concept I was familiar with. What was new to me was that a related event could hold all that pain, anguish and longing that I thought would be attached directly to my sister's passing.

All those difficult feelings relating to her death that I thought I had worked through had somehow managed to make the transition and hide away elsewhere. I clearly hadn't been ready to let them go and hid them well.

The kid brain did an amazing job at hiding them. And nobody had ever thought to have me look at other (possibly related) memories from around the same time – nor would I have ever thought this one to be relevant. I'm not ready to share what it was, nor do I think it really matters.

So far when I discovered something or healed a particular wound. Like when I figured out that I was not to blame for my sister's death. Other memories of situations or events that I grew up thinking were my fault started appearing quite randomly. That one realization helped me change my perspective on about ten other situations. That was the process as I knew it.

This one was different. This was something I thought I had healed from and didn't hold that much weight anymore. I mean just the normal weight that losing somebody will always have, but nothing more than that. I was able to remember my sister by just lighting a candle and taking a moment. Not once did this trigger any emotions that were bigger than expected after what are now more than 44 years.

My kid brain knew that those feelings were too horrible for a five-year-old and hid them away somewhere safe. Somewhere they were safe even if therapists started digging. It never ceases to amaze me. It has so much to teach us about trauma.

15 Resilience does not mean smiling through difficult situations

HARMFUL MISCONCEPTIONS – TIME TO UNDERSTAND

There are stressors all over the place. Different things are stressful for different people. Then there are stressors that are universal. So far, so obvious. Now imagine that something challenging happens. Something that's out of the ordinary, out of your control and entirely unexpected, confusing, potentially traumatic. I don't know a single person who would not find this stressful.

How can we expect people to just keep going the same way they did before? How can we expect people to just shake it off? Well, we can – but it's not a helpful approach.

Taking time to process a situation like that is not a sign of weakness.

- ➢ It's a sign of *taking time to process* - well, duh!
- ➢ It's a sign of knowing that if you deal with it properly in the moment, you take its power away and it won't come back to haunt you.
- ➢ It's a sign of having done the work and of doing your best to navigate life while exercising self-compassion.

Unable to handle stress? No, think again! Processing the emotions that a stressful event triggers IS handling stress. Somehow people have not yet arrived in the 21st century. I don't see it as a badge of honor to just power through and ignore all feelings and emotions. Pretending you're "fine".

Ignoring what's going on, bottling it up is still what we're expected to do. "Happy" is the default setting, right? Happy is what we all need to aspire to. Wrong again!

This is where cognitive dissonance pops into my head. Randomly? Maybe not so much. Recognizing situations that cause cognitive dissonance is also part of handling stress. Staying true to yourself and making decisions that benefit you in the long run is difficult in those situations. It needs practice and it also needs to be possible in the moment. Remember: there's no point or long-term benefit in doing something just to keep the peace.

Robots anyone?

We all know those pictures where you have to decide which of them contain a traffic light, a motorcycle or whatever. All just to prove you are not - in fact - a robot. So, we're having to prove that we're not a machine to a machine. Yet, when we turn out NOT to be a robot that just keeps going no matter what, we're not resilient, we're unable to handle stress.

Sure, makes total sense …

Come on! We need to do better than that. We are human beings. We have emotions. Some need longer to process than others, but all of them are important signals our body sends us. Ignoring them is never helpful. Neither is smiling through the process. I choose to acknowledge all emotions and deal with them in a caring manner. It's called self-compassion or self-care.

I'm not obliged to smile through crappy situations just to make others feel better. Actually, that would not be helpful at all, that would hinder the process.

Think before you tell people to smile more.

16 Feeling safe in today's hate filled world

SAFE? SAFE! – TIME TO UNDERSTAND

It's not always easy. Society's worldview has a hard time keeping up with a changing world.

Change is hard. Changes in your personal life take time and for an entire society to change – well, that takes even longer. I mean if I look at my life growing up, it was simpler in a way. But it was also very black and white. You were either a boy or a girl and that was that. Boys loved girls and girls loved boys. A family was mom, dad and at least two children. You were obviously meant to get married before having them. The mom stayed home with the kids. The dad had a career and brought home the money. Household chores were firmly in female hands. And in the case of Switzerland when I was born women had only just gotten the right to vote. And no, I'm not that old. Switzerland was just insanely and embarrassingly late.

Is it difficult to keep up with the speed at which the world is changing? Well, yes. It is for me at least. I never had to worry about using the correct pronouns to address or talk about a person. I will happily do it, but it does not come naturally - yet. Gender identities? Difficult to grasp if you're not affected yourself. That's a lot of learning and listening to do. At the very least we need to open our minds to a non-binary world with more colors than just black and white and more numbers than just zeros and ones. Accepting other people for who they are doesn't require us to relate to their story. We can be kind. We can listen.

There are groups of people that are finding their voice when their voice is starting to be heard. We as a society need to figure out how to be inclusive and adapt our - at times - very narrow societal norms so everybody feels safe. It's a long ignored human right – not a new invention. Article three of the Universal Declaration of Human Rights states that "Everyone has the right to life, liberty and security of person". It was adopted in 1948. Feeling safe is a human right; one that is being trampled upon by people fueled by hate.

Hate of people who are "different". Hate of people who live a life we don't understand. Hate of people who possibly live a life we can't or won't live. Hate for lifestyles we don't understand. Hate for things that scare us. Hate for anything and anyone we don't understand.

Yes, we crave the feeling of belonging to a group but wouldn't a society that accepts everybody, that is inclusive, do just that? If everybody feels like they belong, isn't that something worth striving for?

And how about we all do the same for ourselves? Feeling safe in our bodies, feeling safe in our minds. Not hating ourselves because of some long held core beliefs. I realize that for some of us (me included) a major mind shift is needed to achieve that.

17 An easy way out – wtaf?!

SOCIETY SUCKS! - TIME TO UNDERSTAND

And society just keeps piling it on. People are traumatized and victim blamed. People reach their breaking point and unalive themselves. And then it's called "the easy way out". Time to understand that it is anything but.

Easy? Looks like there are still people who comment under obituaries that mention suicide that this person took "the easy way out". What the actual fuck? Let's just think about this for a minute. There are people out there who think that feeling so lonely and hopeless that the only option you see for yourself is suicide, is somehow easy? Really?! EASY is the word you want to go for? I don't even have words for how messed up this is. There is a person who is at their lowest, who has given up any hope of life improving or even just their pain getting better, who feels lonely in their struggle, who sees no other way than to end their lives and somebody out there thinks this is EASY. There's so much wrong with that statement. There's so much toxicity in that statement, and so much of what's wrong in this world.

Weak? I got triggered even more when I saw a reel on Instagram where men were asked who they call when they are at their lowest. The answer was – NOBODY, because they are not allowed to show "weakness".

Take a minute.

At their lowest they can't call or tell anybody. What are we even doing to each other? There's nothing weak about talking about your mental health, nothing! But there's a lot wrong in a society where you are told to just suck it up, where your struggle is invalidated because others have it so much worse, where you are called weak, where you have to wait months to be seen by a psychologist/psychiatrist.

Why is there still so much stigma attached to mental health struggles? It can happen to anyone. Yes, ANYone. Yet people are having to hide it because of the stigma attached, because it's not okay to talk about where they are, because they think they are weak, because they were taught to suffer in silence. This makes me sad, angry and everything in between. We, as a society, need to do better! We have to.

Kindness matters. It's not hard to do - and it's free. Try it today!

How about reaching out to a friend? How about being kind to a random stranger? How about giving somebody the gift of a smile? How about sending a kind message to somebody? How about checking in with yourself? How are YOU doing today?

And, there might be family members and friends reading this who have tried their best to help. Please know that it is not always possible. Gentle hugs to you.

18 Keeping the peace?

If you're the kind of person who was told to stay silent to keep the peace, think about whose peace you've been keeping. Most likely not yours. Chances are you were told to stay silent to protect whoever said it. I can't even begin to tell you what that does to a person long term. And that's why I refuse to play that game.

You are ALWAYS allowed to tell your own story. Nobody can silence you. If you're a "yes, but …" person, I know there are legal exceptions. That's not what I'm talking about. I'm talking normal day-to-day living and working.

I have written about gaslighting separately, but this is part of that game too. Along with "nobody will believe you if you tell them". In that case it's likely that a web of lies has already been spun.

It's not always possible to speak up. There are circumstances that don't allow us to, especially when we're young and still living at home. We can still understand that our silence is keeping the peace of others. And understand that only people who don't want to take responsibility for their own actions will tell you to stay quiet. If they ask for your forgiveness and your silence at the same time – what does that tell you?

They're not going to change.

You are in control of your own story. Nobody can take that away from you. The people who are trying to silence you are afraid of your voice. They are scared to be found out. They are scared that their abuse will become public. They are scared that they have to own up and take responsibility for their actions. They are scared.

Understanding that I am not responsible for other people's actions and that this peace I've been keeping was a way of avoiding conflict – a way of avoiding conflict for them – that was a huge milestone for me. So, when this pattern occurs today with consequences threatened – I get triggered. And this happens:

39

I'm seriously fed up with people telling me what I can and cannot talk about. That's keeping their peace, that's protecting them. So, to protect myself and to keep my own peace, I speak up.

> Don't tell me to be quiet – I won't.
>
> Don't tell me it will keep the peace – not my peace.
>
> Don't tell me to protect others with my silence – I'm protecting myself by speaking up.
>
> Don't tell me you had no other choice – you won't get validation from me.
>
> Don't tell me vulnerability is a sign of weakness – it's a sign of strength.
>
> Don't tell me I'm too sensitive – I'm not a robot.
>
> Don't tell me you're protecting others – you're only protecting yourself.
>
> Don't lie – we both know the truth.
>
> Don't think I don't know – I do.
>
> Don't think I can't see – I can.
>
> Don't think I'll be quiet – I won't.
>
> Don't play the victim – you're not.

If people didn't want others to know how they treated you, they should have treated you better. It's that simple.

19 You are not alone!

WHO CARES? – TIME TO UNDERSTAND

We need to understand that so many people suffer in silence. At least some of them because they think that they are alone in what they're going through and that nobody cares. Let's change that! And we also need to understand that nobody is always "fine". Nobody! Remember that.

I grew up in an environment where mental health or even feelings in general were not something you'd talk about. Steep learning curve later on, I can tell you. What I found was that the more I talked about trauma and mental health with friends, acquaintances, or colleagues, the more I got that feeling of "I'm not alone". Or "wow, I was not expecting that, they seem so happy". Those were eye-opening moments.

I was under the impression that I had to be "fine" all the time. Especially when I lived in the US. I got asked about 100x a day "Hi, how are you today?". I know it's really just a rhetorical question. Or not even a question, more of a greeting. And you don't react honestly. The answer is usually "fine, how are you?". You also say this when all you want to do is go lie down and have a cry. We'll leave this random greeting version aside for now. It's not helpful. PERIOD.

Try this next time you're feeling a bit down and a friend or colleague asks you how you are doing: "Actually, not doing great today" or any variation that works for you. You might be surprised. I certainly was when a cup of tea and some chocolates suddenly appeared on my desk or people stopped for a quick chat just to check in.

People are generally kind. It's safe to let them know. It does take a whole lot of courage though. And it's not always possible. Be gentle with yourself when you try it. The "simple" act of being real could trigger something. Not a reason not to try, just something to be aware of.

Having said all that, let's focus on how we're all basically trying to survive and not kill anybody on a daily basis. Maybe I'm just speaking for myself, but people can be a real pain.

How do we make up for that? I mean we are all in this thing called "life" together, so we kind of have to find a way to make it work, right? A very helpful piece of advice I got was to remember to do something fun every day. I immediately protested: "I do fun stuff!". Then I thought about it some more.

I realized that I didn't. I did things that I enjoyed, but FUN – silly, giggling like a little kid kind of fun? Nope, I did not. And it's also not as easy as it sounds. But as a friend of mine likes to remind me "silliness is important". If we can be silly together, we can get through tough times together too. Understanding this and talking about feelings have shown me that I am not alone and that some people are actually pretty damn great.

Remember that. Now go do something silly!

20 You have a broken finger? Suck it up!

GASLIGHTING – TIME TO UNDERSTAND

You would never say that to a friend who has a broken finger, would you? Then why do I keep hearing people say this exact thing when friends are struggling with their mental health?

Yes, there are much worse injuries than a broken finger. I think we can agree on that. But does this mean that the broken finger does not need to be looked at? I think we would also agree that this isn't the case. What we don't need to hear is that we should be thankful about the broken finger because look at Tommy he broke his entire arm or shoulder or leg. That isn't helpful at all.

Yet, we do it when it comes to mental health. We tell people to be grateful that they are not in Tommy's shoes.

We've established that it's a minor injury – as injuries go. But there might be some hidden damage, or it could be a very complicated fracture and tendons could be affected too. Also, remember the joints? You might lose function in one of those.

In this case because it was a physical injury the finger was seen by a doctor quite quickly and the healing process started.

If we're struggling with our mental health and we're constantly being told to be grateful, to be happy, to look on the bright side without anybody taking things seriously, where does that leave us? Are we ourselves going to take those feelings seriously when we should clearly just be grateful that we're not dealing with "real" trauma?

Could we please stop doing this? It's so very harmful. And it IS the same as telling a friend with a broken finger to suck it up.

I meet too many people who think their problems are not big enough for them to even talk about - because there's so many others who have it a lot

43

worse. How is that solving any problems? I will continue to let people know that they are not alone. And I will continue to let people know when I'm having a shit day. Because guess what?! Those happen. They are normal. Not talking about them doesn't make them magically disappear, does it? Yet we've normalized pretending to be okay – always.

Can you call in sick where you are and officially take a mental health day? Or do you call in sick with a cold, headache etc. instead? I would love to see mental health days becoming a thing here. And to those of you saying that people would abuse such a system - are you the ones who would? Is that how you know?

And then there's this: I hurt myself (I might or might not be responsible for the injury), now I need physio – perfectly okay. Good for you. People messed me up during childhood (most definitely not responsible for the damage caused) now I need psychotherapy – big problem. Because "is your problem really big enough for therapy"?

I get triggered by people being told to suck it up because there are people with real trauma – I will always speak up when I hear this. It's too important a topic. It's too harmful a thing to say. It's gaslighting at its worst.

21 Forgiving myself? Not so fast!

FORGIVENESS – TIME TO UNDERSTAND

Let me start by sharing how this story came about. I bought a book on December 23, 2022. It was a German crime novel that took place on an island in the North Sea. I thought it looked interesting. There might have been a lighthouse on the cover. There was nothing to indicate that it might contain a trigger of any kind. The story was well written, and I enjoyed reading it. Then there was this little boy. He was four years old and got blamed for his brother's disappearance and subsequent death. Major trigger! Just how major I didn't know at the time.

The funny thing about triggers is that you never know where/how they find you. In this case it reminded me of certain events that happened when I was between four and six. I realized that I was blaming myself for much of it. That little boy in the story was clearly way too young to be responsible for anything that happened in his life at that time, but I in turn was most definitely to blame for everything that happened in my life when I was four. Our brain is weird that way. Realizing that a four-year-old can't be held responsible for events in their lives was an important steppingstone.

This trigger helped me realize that I had this internalized guilt. I was the reason my sister died. Don't get me wrong. I've known for decades that a genetic defect caused her death. I took genetics classes at uni and knew that my parents had a 25% chance of losing a child to this specific genetic disorder. Four kids – one died; the math sadly works out perfectly.

And now to the important part. Every child aged five whose mother is pregnant is bound to bump into her tummy at some point. A mom's natural reaction might be "be careful, you don't want to hurt the baby" or "you're hurting the baby". Normally, the baby is born healthy, and they live happily ever after.

Now picture this … the baby is born, it's not healthy and dies a few weeks later. Suddenly, those words take on a completely different meaning. I'm responsible for my sister's death. I hurt her when she was inside my mom's belly. That was my kid brain's reality.

> ➤ To five-year old me this explanation made perfect sense.

> ➤ Five-year old me did not have the vocabulary to express or understand my feelings. I just wanted to run away and hide in shame.

> ➤ As a five-year-old I unknowingly bottled up that guilt and kept as quiet as I could so people wouldn't find out.

> ➤ Five-year old me didn't mourn my sister's death. I didn't want to make my parents even sadder by crying.

How do you come back from this? By understanding biology – and then by understanding that it's impossible for a five-year old to fully comprehend actions and consequences.

So, what did I need to forgive myself for? My kid brain did the best it could trying to protect me. Full points for that. I needed to let go of feeling responsible for something I was not responsible for. That's different from forgiveness. Forgiveness is only needed when you did something wrong.

I didn't.

Milestone realization.

22 The kid brain

HEALING TRAUMA – TIME TO UNDERSTAND

I've developed a kind of love/hate relationship with my kid brain. I love how it protected me and made decisions and connections well beyond its age. It was absolutely brilliant and I'm super proud. What is also was and still is, is a huge pain in the you know what. It still thinks it needs to protect me. It makes me hold on to harmful beliefs that really have no place in an adult person's life.

Here is how I understand the kid brain. Oh and I'm calling it that because I can never remember the proper names of things and it works well for my message. Our brain is amazing in analyzing the world around us. When we're very young there are many exciting things going on and the brain is firing on all cylinders all the time. It analyses every gesture, every word and the context is soaked up too. I mean, we're there to learn and that's exactly how we learn.

Initially we don't have a concept of other people influencing our environment. When somebody comes home angry, we assume it was something we did. The same is true if somebody is happy – that was us. This is developmentally normal. What else are we going to think? We can't leave our little family bubble and go explore - yet. If I remember correctly from my child development psych class children start recognizing themselves in the mirror at around 15 months. Milestone.

When we're around four or five we start understanding that we are an individual person and that that's how others perceive us. All this is going on while our kid brain is trying to make sense of the world. Now, what tripped me up was the fact that our kid brain doesn't seem to distinguish between behavior and self.

So, if you tell a kid that they did something bad and leave it at that, they will internalize that they themselves are a bad person. Again, this is a normal thing for the kid brain to do. However, I am still untangling this way of thinking decades later. Taking a step back and looking at the behavior I don't like and not equaling it to hating myself. Yikes! You wouldn't believe how much effort that takes.

Hating a bad habit instead of hating myself, what a milestone that was. And yes, this was my kid brain still telling me that if I eat "bad" food, I'm a bad person. It was also telling me that if I did something "bad", I was a terrible person. And by "bad" I mean undesired, which in turn makes me an undesirable person. Do you see the pattern? This ran incredibly deep. And was directly linked to my sense of self, my worthiness and me questioning my place in this world. Very deep!

The kid brain also tries to take responsibility for everything. At least mine did. It wants to fix everything and everybody and overanalyzes things that don't need analyzing. If you go back to the "I'm the center of the universe and everything revolves around me" view of the world. This makes perfect sense.

It is our caregivers who can help us develop a healthier sense of age-appropriate responsibility and self-worth. They need to be emotionally mature to be able to do just that. And trust me when I say that this is not a given at all.

23 Is it even possible?

THE DREAM – TIME TO UNDERSTAND

Understanding how dreams work, wouldn't that be wonderful? I don't think anybody can ever really know, but here's how it felt for me. You're gonna hate me saying "anything is possible", aren't you? Well, you know. I do think it is. There are just too many things I was conditioned to believe could never happen that have - in fact - happened.

I know that I haven't told you what that big dream of mine was and I'm not sure it's important for you to know. And before I consider telling you, I would like you to ask yourselves "what is my dream?" one more time. Remember that there are no restrictions at all. It doesn't matter if you can't afford that dream. It doesn't matter if you are married or in a relationship and your dream doesn't include that partner. It doesn't matter if it feels ridiculous to even say it. Just go with it! Open your mind to the possibility and see what happens. Don't think about it too much, just say whatever comes to mind. At the very least thinking about your dream will make you smile and that is never a bad thing.

It starts with positive what ifs. I'll keep mentioning those until you start believing it. Planting that seed of what if this is possible. And then possibly daydream about it. A lot.

A tree might not magically appear tomorrow, but a seed is a seed. Your next decisions may subconsciously also factor in that dream. It's a fascinating process. It really is. For that seed to take you'll need the right people in your life. People who don't laugh at your dreams. People who encourage you. People who support you. People who believe in you. People who know that dreams are important. People who want to see you happy. People who want you to succeed. We could also call them friends. The real kind. The *I'll stay up with you until I know you're okay* kind.

You might have already tentatively done things that moved towards the dream. I mean I had a travel blog and enjoyed writing about my adventures.

My friends loved those stories. I always had anecdotes to share and as much fun writing them as my friends had reading them. Things just flowed.

I never felt like I had anything really worthwhile to say, so I abandoned the idea of writing a book. I mean, I knew I didn't have the patience of sitting down and coming up with a plot and characters. To me writing a book was always a novel. I mean, what else could I write?

Did my dream care? Nope, that's not how dreams work. I was encouraged to write by the universe. I always came back to it but didn't know how. I tried extending my travel blog with daily posts. That didn't take. Only when I started writing on Substack on a regular basis, did I find my voice. My voice grew as I started writing. Writing about random things. Rants were my favorites but also mental health matters. I started a second newsletter when I felt I had important and trauma related topics to talk about.

There was a second part to my dream that only a few people know about. I'm now curious how I'm gonna make that happen. It's a seed that was planted in primary school and it's taking its time. That's how dreams start – with a seed.

Trust the process and watch it grow.

24 I CAN make changes

It really just takes one single person to believe you can do it for you to start believing it as well. I'm proof positive of that. And I'm also very much a work in progress. The biggest change was starting over entirely on my own during a global pandemic. Let's start with something easy, shall we?

That step was incredibly difficult, but necessary. I knew that. I also knew I could do it. I knew that deep down. And this is when doubts started creeping in anyway. Would I really be able to live on my own? Would I be okay? Continued support from friends helped me go for it.

And you know what? Change is possible. Who knew? You all probably did, but I needed to learn that. Was it difficult at times? – of course. Did I doubt whether I had made the right decision? Well, not really. In this case it was the right decision from the start.

I said that I am very much still a work in progress and I really am. And with that huge and very successful change firmly under my belt, I could start knocking some other ones out of the park. Like becoming an artist, a hiking ambassador and a writer. Why the hell not?

I used to focus too much on my failed attempts and feel stuck in undesired habits. But if we look at how habits are formed and how we learn, every single failed attempt is a step forward. If we let it.

I'll give you an example. Let's say you want to stop eating potato chips – not sure why you would, but bear with me. You've successfully not eaten any on nine occasions where you wanted to but then the 10th one comes around, and you cave. You won't be focusing on the nine successful attempts, you'll be devastated by the 10th. This was so totally me.

Now if you think about a little baby who is learning to walk. It walked nine steps and then falls on its bum, what would you say? Would you berate it for not walking any further? Would you tell it it was useless? Would you tell it how disappointed you were? No? Then why are you telling yourself all those things?

New level unlocked. Positive self-talk. If you tell yourself "Great effort. Now get up and try again!" instead of "you're useless, you failed again", how would that change things? Actually believing we can makes all the difference. We tend to believe in others far more than we believe in ourselves. That's something we can change.

I'm gonna come at you with the positive "what ifs" again. What if it does work out? What if you do make it? What if it's even better than you could ever have imagined? What if you CAN do it? How wonderful would that feel?

Pretty freaking wonderful, I can tell you that. I never believed I could and now I am doing it.

STEP III: TIME TO RETHINK CORE BELIEFS

25 Feelings are gifts

FEELINGS – TIME TO RETHINK CORE BELIEFS

You can either accept them or ignore them. You can embrace them or throw them away. Feelings are not good or bad. This is such a harmful core belief. I'll tell you why. Your kid brain cannot distinguish between having a "good" feeling and being "good" or having a "bad" feeling and being "bad". It automatically thinks that if I have a bad feeling, I'm a bad person.

You can easily check if you hold this core belief. You might feel jealous because a friend is doing something you've always wanted to do but haven't. What do you do? Where does your brain go? If it tells you not to feel jealous because this is your friend and you should be happy for them, you might want to consider a rethink.

Jealousy is bad, right? We were all taught that. Follow the steps from a previous chapter. Acknowledge that you are feeling jealous. No judgement. Approach it with a sense of wonderment or curiosity - if you can. I wonder why I'm feeling jealous. This is interesting.

And yes, you can feel super happy for someone but feel jealous at the same time. How about looking at this as a sign of things you'd like to do yourself. A sign of wanting to grow and dare to do something new. A sign of being stuck in a life you'd like to change. A sign of longing to be able to make the necessary changes in your own life.

There might also be a feeling of resentment. Somebody is successful in something you've always wanted to do, and you think you're better at it than them anyway. And it's not fair that this is not happening for you. All normal. Look at it as a big, huge signpost pointing you in the direction of your dream(s). And go get them.

It's all a matter of perspective and interpretation. All feelings matter. Every single emotion is there for a reason. We don't have to react; we don't even have to like them – they are there either way. Feeling bad about how we feel and pushing feelings away is never going to point us in the right direction. We need to stay with them for that to happen.

How about looking at every feeling as a gift? There are gifts we like and keep. Then there are others we receive, look at, evaluate and don't keep around. They might even get thrown out or regifted. The important thing is to receive them, acknowledge their existence explicitly and then decide if they are useful to us at this point in time. You can't change the way you feel, but you can – to a certain extent – decide how to handle your emotions in any given moment.

Dwelling on negative feelings with a bucket of ice cream might be the thing to do one day and the next day you can examine the feeling more closely and understand why it had been there in the first place. This will take away its power.

Feelings are powerful gifts – use them wisely.

26 You don't have any trauma? What if …

UNDERSTANDING TRAUMA – TIME TO RETHINK CORE BELIEFS

… we call it unprocessed memories? All of us have those. I don't think it's possible to make it through life without picking up at least a couple. So, what are they?

Picture this, you're sitting in a classroom and the teacher makes a remark to you that has your classmates snickering. Could be something simple like "did you remember to feed our class guinea pig?" And you had in fact forgotten about feeding it. This was easily rectified and that could have been the end of it.

Your classmates snickering because you made a mistake stuck with you though. You tried to do everything perfectly from then on, so as not to repeat this. And you were really hard on yourself.

Your perfectionism was born, and the slightest mistake triggered a fear response in you. One of people laughing.

Years later this one experience can still hold you back without you realizing it. You don't walk around telling people that you're afraid to make a mistake because of a class guinea pig in 4th grade. Mostly, because you don't know.

And there are many such experiences in childhood.

In an ideal world every time something like this happens the child would realize it, tell an adult who could then help them process the incident and the attached feelings. That doesn't feel very realistic though. I mean we are expecting very young children to communicate complex emotions triggered by everyday occurrences. Unrealistic.

We also expect parents and other adults in children's lives to be very tuned into what can happen on a regular (school) day and ask precisely the right questions at the right time. Unrealistic.

My point is that it's impossible to achieve.

Apart from the obvious big T Trauma, these seemingly tiny wounds can go unnoticed for decades. During that time, similar injuries are added. Those new injuries are both burying the initial wound deeper and adding to it.

And that's why we can get to a point where we feel stuck or frustrated with certain situations happening over and over again; with specific habits that we just can't seem to change, even though we managed with so many others; with having the same argument over and over again.

Depending how deep those memories and respective wounds are buried it will need a lot of practice or professional help to access them.

We all have those unprocessed memories. You can picture them like nameless files you quickly saved to your desktop. At some point you will need to open and look at them to decide where to put them or if you even still need them. You will need to go back to them unless you remember what "document1111" was and can delete or move it without checking what it was again. Now if you look at each of them individually and put it in the correct folder - you're firmly on the right track.

With that awareness, we end up with tools for everyday life. Tools such as:

> Noticing triggers.
> Examining feelings.
> Healing wounds by bringing them to the surface.
> Changing our perspective on core beliefs.
> Putting memories where they belong once they are processed.

We all have unprocessed traumatic memories in our lives, every single one of us. We're on this journey together.

27 It's not a freaking competition!

HARMFUL MISCONCEPTIONS – TIME TO RETHINK CORE BELIEFS

This one happens too frequently, and it irritates me so much. When I started talking about childhood trauma, I was often told that "Others have/had it much worse than you!" and basically to just suck it up. This is a big one for me. I mean, COME ON – tell me: who has the worst trauma then? Who is allowed to feel bad and struggle with the trauma they suffered? There can clearly be only one if we're going by the "others have it worse" rule.

This is another way of invalidating what you're feeling. Others have it worse? How is that a helpful response? It just tells people "you don't matter!" or "your feelings don't matter". Can we please stop that? I can only deal with my own trauma and my own emotions. I need to heal my own personal trauma – everybody does. I can empathize of course, but my personal trauma is the only one I CAN heal.

Why is this so important to me?

The people who talk like that most likely invalidate their own feelings as well. They are grateful [insert: for what happened to them] because it could have been worse. If that "insert" bothers you – I'm glad I have your attention now. Being told to be grateful instead of working through your struggles - I don't even know what to say about that. That's just seriously messed up.

I'll tell you what – you matter!

Who knew? I matter! Taking care of others – yes, I got that down. It's also a good escape. Having to deal with yourself is not always easy. I've started to "disappoint" others instead of myself. Wow! That's a steep learning curve. Doing what's best for you and people are disappointed, because you're not going out of your way to meet THEIR needs and they get annoyed.

Well, there's a message in that – be honest about your needs and communicate them openly. See what happens.

Also, take your time to process things. Everybody processes feelings at their own rate. Again, this is not a competition. There's no prize for whoever processes difficult emotions the fastest. I sometimes get tired of people looking at mental health as a competition. Yes, I've gotten faster at processing things, but that just means that I've had a lot of shit to process to get here. It is not something I wish on anybody. I really don't.

There are things that need time and also practice. So, you start practicing and start going where it hurts where feelings are trapped and society goes "you should be grateful you have such an easy life" – can we agree that this is not helpful? It doesn't matter how seemingly small somebody's struggle feels to you. It's their struggle. And it takes a hell of a lot of courage to go where it hurts and to start healing.

Don't dismiss other people's struggles. You have no way of knowing what's going on. And the next person who tells me to be grateful – well, you've been warned.

28 Shifting the hate within

It's difficult to feel safe in a hate filled world. Especially if one doesn't fit societal norms. I stand by everything I say in the "Society sucks" chapters. And all this fueled the hate within me. Apparently, there are so many things wrong with me. We're all told to love ourselves yet everywhere we look we see reasons not to. This doesn't make any sense and social media are not making things any easier. Now we're also fighting the algorithms.

So, what's going on inside our brain with all this? Let me try to explain. When you have that kid brain that's interpreting the world around you in the only way it can, namely taking everything personally and internalizing presumed facts, you run into trouble later. If society thinks I'm not a real girl because I don't play with dolls there must be something fundamentally wrong with me. If I'm told to be quiet and not speak up, I must not have anything important to say. When I want to hug somebody and get pushed away time and time again, I must be unlovable. When I try everything to be loved but get nothing in return, I must be a complete failure that's undeserving of life.

Stuff like that had been going on in my brain. I was aware of some of it as those are known patterns. However, that knowledge didn't help me heal. It should do. I mean once you start realizing that these patterns are there, things should improve, right?

Well, sometimes they do but other times there are associated feelings that run very deep, and you need to find a way to access those. What I found in my case was self-hatred. There was so much of it and it was such an intense feeling that I could really feel it in every fiber of my body. I even managed to access what felt like the initial wound. The feeling seemed to work its way through my entire body and then release itself through my legs and feet.

I'm not actually sure if this was the end of it or if I need to go a couple of more rounds. All I know is that even though I didn't sleep more than three hours, I felt completely energized the next day. I even managed a pre-work run. Something I'd never done in my life.

I think I'm on the right track.

Just to recap: your kid brain does an amazing job analyzing your surroundings and keeping you safe when you're young. It holds on to those beliefs way into adulthood unless you are taught to unlearn them, and your kid brain trusts that you are safe. Otherwise, it stays in survival mode and continues to make unhelpful assumptions.

As a child it is important to analyze our surroundings and it can be crucial for our survival to conform to societal norms, accept not being loved the way you need to be, always put our own needs second and to read a room perfectly and adapt our behavior accordingly. That's all very helpful at the time. What's not so helpful is the underlying feelings I described above. Those need to be reprocessed in our brain and released from our nervous system.

Only a body and mind that have come out of survival mode can feel safe. I'm getting there. Step by step. Feeling by feeling.

29 Society taught me what?!

SOCIETY SUCKS! - TIME TO RETHINK CORE BELIEFS

Where do I even start? I mean I was taught that not wanting to have kids is bad. Having kids is my purpose in life – or so I'm told. Why would I have to explain and/or defend my decision not to want children to anyone? How is that anybody else's business? Also, no need to defend your own decision to have kids. You do you!

As a woman this is so deeply ingrained. I can't even tell you how long it took me to realize I didn't have to conform. I never wanted kids.

Then I figured out that "no" is a perfectly fine answer to the question "do you have kids?". I mean it's a yes/no question. Why would you expect a more expansive answer? And then I also learned that people don't really want to hear my extensive list of reasons why I don't have kids. Funny that! They just want to tell me what I'm missing and why I should absolutely have kids. Sometimes I do have a bit of fun with that discussion, I will admit to that. I'm evil that way.

And no, asking a family member if they want kids or why they don't want kids is no better than if it's a stranger. None of your business! Period! If somebody wants to talk about it, they will. Seriously! I got asked that question at every single family gathering between the ages of 20ish and 41 (that's when I stopped going). I was letting everybody down! I was the oldest granddaughter and daughter after all. Asking them to stop didn't really help either.

There was a biological clock and was I aware of that? I am now picturing THAT scene from *My Cousin Vinny* and laughing. Oh, and I was gonna regret my decision. Haven't yet and I'm 49.

Then the kids are here, and we immediately go pink or blue. How is pink and blue even still a thing? And don't get me started on gender reveals ...

You know those Kinder Surprise Eggs? In Switzerland we have two versions – a blue one and a pink one. I recently witnessed a little girl crying because she was given a blue one. There was a dinosaur inside and the person who gave it to her knew that she liked dinosaurs. Took me forever to calm her down and explain to her that girls can play with dinosaurs and that the blue and pink colors didn't matter. This is 2024 and we are still telling our kids that pink is for girls and blue is for boys and that they are not allowed to play with toys that don't correspond to their gender.

I mean toy stores have pink and blue sections. Okay, they might not actually be pink and blue, but there's a girl's and a boy's section. How is this a helpful concept? And while I'm here, why do we need a word for a girl that doesn't conform to society's gender norms? Is there a male equivalent to "tomboy"? If there is, I can't think of one right now.

Those society-taught core beliefs run deep, and they keep being reaffirmed. Toxic!

I'm working on becoming an unapologetically childless tomboy version of a middle-aged woman and society can go – you know what – itself.

30 Screw toxic positivity and embrace life!

Someone said: "it's entirely up to you whether you want to be happy – you just have to decide to be happy". **Where do I even start? I seriously don't know. That's toxic positivity at its best – or rather at its worst.** You can't just happy your way out of everything. And yes, that is me using "happy" as a verb.

Toxic positivity causes feelings of shame and guilt. It promotes avoidance and denial. And ultimately causes a lot of pain. I can't even begin to tell you how crucial it is to stop with this toxic positivity BS. It destroys lives – and I mean that literally. It almost cost me mine. Toxic positivity tells you that your feelings are not valid. That you're doing something wrong if you can't make yourself feel happy. That uncomfortable feelings are bad – we mustn't have them. All this is preventing us from healing, from growing, from living ...

Another favorite of mine is that you can find something positive in every situation. Why? Why would I spend time looking for a positive aspect of let's say my sister's death? Why would I waste time on that? It sucked! That's it. It was horrible. It was traumatic. It took years of working through what had become complicated grief because at the time I didn't grieve. I was trying to make everybody happy by being happy.

There are everyday situations that are difficult and you can't just happy your way out of them. That's life. Pretending you're happy in such situations – come on! Talk about cognitive dissonance. How about acknowledging "this sucked/sucks" and go from there? Acknowledgement is what's key here.

Also, how boring would life be if "happy" was our only setting? Very boring! That's what it would be. But if we all felt happy and only happy all the time, boring or bored wouldn't even be an option.

I'm all for strategies that help you manage your emotions; that keep you from downward spiraling; that help you get out of a funk quicker; that change your perspective on something. You can't control your thoughts. You can't control your feelings. That's just not possible.

You can shift your focus. You can change your perspective. You can look for positive things around you to help you manage difficult emotions at that time. But you can also grab a bucket of ice cream and hide under your covers for a day, because sometimes life or people just suck. And you definitely do not have to be happy about that.

I realized during my walks that now that I let myself feel all those emotions I'd been trying to avoid for so long, it is easier for me to express them too. I might not always find the right word, but I can describe what I'm feeling much better. It's all connected.

I am much happier now that I'm not pretending to be happy all the time.

31 Inner child? – Think again!

WHO CARES? – TIME TO RETHINK CORE BELIEFS

Let me tell you how my trauma healing started when I stopped trying to heal that *inner child*. I'm suggesting a change of focus: heal yourself. In the here and now.

Picture this: You're struggling with something. Could be self-worth, could be feeling like you're not good enough. I mean there are endless possibilities and I'm not giving you a list of things to feel bad about. Sorry, you'll have to do that yourselves. For this example, just pick one that you can relate to.

One version of healing your inner child is sitting in front of a mirror talking to it. Now, here's why I find this unhelpful.

One of the things that can happen with childhood trauma is that you dissociate. That's a survival mechanism. If you boil it down to an emotional detachment from reality or your surroundings because it's too difficult – that makes perfect sense. It's very necessary in that moment.

That's step one.

Consider a situation where you're struggling for some reason. Let's say you feel like you're not appreciated, and this is a feeling you know all too well. It's really getting you down and since you learned about healing your *inner child* you give this a try. You remove yourself from your present situation, you talk to your inner child, you cry, you hug, you wipe your tears and then you go back to where you were before.

Step out – step back. Now to me, this feels like dissociation. Massively so.

What I had to learn during my (trauma) healing journey was to NOT dissociate in emotionally difficult situations and stay present. This doesn't only concern big T trauma (i.e. what everybody would consider trauma), but any emotion that is difficult to deal with.

If you're struggling in the here and now, this is where you need to stay. YOU have these feelings, and you have them NOW. Stay with them, feel them, practice feeling them even - and especially - if it's hard. Your *inner child* is not struggling right now YOU are! Reconnecting with yourself and your feelings is what is needed. YOU are hurting. YOU need to heal. Here. Now.

Yes, but … childhood experiences matter.

Of course they do. And I'll be the first one to say that. It's where it all started. It's where we learned how to regulate our emotions, how to express them or less ideally how to dissociate from them and hide them away. Also, consider this – YOU have struggled since childhood. YOU were hurt as a child. This hurt has been with you for a long time. If it affects your life in the here and now, it needs to be dealt with in the here and now.

> ➢ **YOU were hurt as a child (past)**
> ➢ **YOU struggle now (present)**
> ➢ **YOU have struggled since childhood (present perfect – ongoing up to now)**

You don't need to go back to your childhood to learn how to regulate your current emotions. Those feelings are still around for a reason. The answer will eventually lie in realizing how old those feelings are and after a bit of work – letting them go.

There have been so many books written on *healing your inner child* that my approach might be controversial. However, when I realized that the *inner child* was not a separate entity to work with and started working with my current self – that's when the healing began.

Remember that YOU matter in the here and NOW.

32 What advice would you give your younger self?

GASLIGHTING – TIME TO RETHINK CORE BELIEFS

I used to play the *what advice would you give your younger self* game. Be it on social media, be it in real life. I had my go-to answer. It was *dare to be yourself*. I think the game limited your advice to five words or less.

So, let's talk about why *dare to be yourself* is no longer my answer and why I find it harmful now. It implies that I did something wrong when I was younger. It implies that if I had done things differently my life would somehow be better now. It implies that I wasn't enough the way I was.

Yet, I did what I had to - to survive. Being myself had literally and figuratively been knocked out of me. How is *dare to be yourself* helpful here? It really isn't. I did exactly what I had to. I was a tough little girl. A real fighter. Not somebody you want to mess with as a 49-year-old either.

Would my life be better if I'd dared to be myself? Again, there's no way of knowing. I do think, however, that I would have been broken even more and would not have made it to 49. So, I'm good with what I did when I was younger. It was brave. It was smart. I knew how to make it through - instinctively.

I said that my answer changed. What would it be now? I think I would not give my younger self advice – she's got things covered. I would tell her:

You are great just the way you are and you're doing an amazing job navigating a complicated situation. The time for you to show your true self and shine will come. Take good care of yourself and don't forget who you truly are until you reach that safe place.

I know what you're gonna say "Evelyne, that's more than five words" – gee, thanks Einstein! Life is complicated and if it fits into a Snapple cap it's probably not helpful or too simplistic.

As a child I was too loud (for a girl), too opinionated (for a girl), too competitive (for a girl), too good at soccer (for a girl), too handy (for a girl), too good at math (for a girl), too smart (for a girl), not girly enough (for a girl), not interested enough in dolls (for a girl). There's probably a lot more, but you get the picture.

Society taught me to tone down my personality. Basically, to hide myself because I was not okay, because I was broken, I was not acceptable.

As adults it is our job to question and challenge those core beliefs. Let's all stop gaslighting ourselves. In case you were wondering, telling our younger selves to *dare to be themselves* or anything else to that effect is in fact gaslighting ourselves.

Language is powerful, we need to be careful how we use it. We need to consider our words. Especially when we're talking to ourselves.

33 Some thoughts on forgiveness and trauma healing

FORGIVENESS – TIME TO RETHINK CORE BELIEFS

Let me start by saying there's only one person you need to forgive to heal your trauma and that's you. That could easily be the end of this chapter, but I know that there are different opinions on this subject out there. How you feel about forgiveness will depend on your upbringing and your faith. So let me walk you through my thoughts on the topic.

So, do you need to forgive the people who hurt you? The short answer is – no, you don't. Does your healing progress any faster if you do? Also no. On the contrary it might actually hinder it to a certain extent.

Let's look at what happens when someone asks for your forgiveness. First, they are basically just acknowledging they hurt you. That's all. But you already knew that. They already knew that. It's a pointless exercise. And then it gets harmful. By forgiving them you are basically saying that you are okay with them treating you that way. It's a trap.

What happened is part of your life - forgiveness can't undo this. Nothing can. And why would the people who hurt you be part of your healing process? A healing process that is needed because of the trauma they caused. Seeing stories where the perpetrator later plays the hero in helping the victims makes me feel sick to my stomach. This is so toxic.

It is my job to heal from the trauma somebody else caused me. And I can forgive myself for how long it took me to realize what was going on. I can forgive myself for the way I let people treat me. I can start building healthy boundaries. All that is on me.

What is not on me is how guilty somebody feels for what they have done. That is their feeling. That is their problem. Repentance – sure, but it needs to come with a change in behavior. How many abusers offend-repent-offend-repent? With their victims staying because they believe it was the last time.

Society needs to stop forcing people to forgive and start focusing on holding the perpetrators to account. People don't think they can break up or get a divorce and stay in toxic situations for too long. I know, I've been there. I managed to turn things around and we are now on good terms. No forgiveness needed. An acknowledgement of previous behavior and a change in that behavior. That's what it took.

I realize that sometimes it's not possible (like if we're too young), or safe to cut people out of your life. We have to wait for the right moment. Hang in there! You got this. And then start working through those toxic patterns and keep working through your pain. Step by step.

People who say you just forgive and move on have no idea what they are talking about. Your healing is not about them or anybody else. It's about you. You got hurt. You need to heal. You can move on without them. You got this! You are important! And you are not alone! Remember that and remember to be gentle with yourself.

34 You can't analyze trauma away

HEALING TRAUMA – TIME TO RETHINK CORE BELIEFS

Everybody who knows me also knows that I'm a very analytical person. I need and want to understand everything. In German we have the expression "Kopfmensch". There doesn't seem to be a corresponding English word, but it basically means that you are in your head a lot. It also implies that you are not very connected to your feelings.

In the past four years I have learned to embrace all emotions. And what a steep learning curve that was! Just picture this person who (over-)analyzes everything being faced with a flood of emotions that want to be heard, seen, acknowledged. It really did feel like a flood - or maybe a big wave that drew me under and had me fight to reach the surface again.

Even though I mostly ride that wave confidently now, there are still moments when I fall off and struggle to come up for air. In those moments it helps to know that I can surf. I just need to get back on the board. This can be difficult. Very difficult. Difficult, yet doable. Exhausting and scary but I've done it before. And I keep reminding myself of that.

Now how does analyzing things play into healing trauma? This is an interesting aspect that does not get talked about enough. We analyze what happened in our past and how it affects us today. There are (text)books that tell you which trauma is likely connected to which underlying emotions. That knowledge isn't a shortcut and doesn't help us heal trauma. It can be part of the overall process, but the actual healing starts when we tap into those underlying feelings.

Picture it as two different systems – there's your analytical brain and there's your emotional brain. Yes, this is very simplified. I'm just trying to make a point. Your analytical brain and your emotional brain don't communicate directly. They are not linked in that way. Your analytical brain can't access the hidden storage of the emotional brain. That's why you can't just analyze your trauma away. You need access to the underlying emotions first.

Then it's like you unlocked a treasure. Going with those emotions and truly feeling them brings them to the surface. They are no longer hidden or scary. Your analytical brain is now able to make sense of things. And your emotional brain is relieved that there is now one less hidden item stored in it. It might also have more capacity to process current emotions and keep them from disappearing into that hidden folder. At least it sometimes feels like that to me.

So, what do you say? Ready to get out of your head and tap into your emotions? It'll be worth it. Just make sure you have tissues and emotional support food ready. You'll need them.

35 Yes, I can!

THE DREAM – TIME TO RETHINK CORE BELIEFS

The core belief of never being able to achieve certain things runs deep. Writing was of course not the only area I was told as a child that I couldn't succeed in. I mean girls were meant to be quiet, maybe get a degree (but why would they), not draw attention to themselves, get married, have children and be housewives. Not much scope for dreams of any kind.

And suddenly I learned to voice my dreams and aspirations. I learned not to worry about people shaking their heads calling me a "dreamer". I learned to ignore all the doubters. Enter my next dream: becoming a famous artist and traveling the world – just living off selling my art. And you know what? I do think I could pull this off too. Seriously, the sky's the limit.

In February or March, I felt this strong impulse to paint. I had no idea what and why. Luckily the shops were already closed, and I couldn't go out and buy painting supplies. A seed had been planted though. I kind of liked art class in school, but I was no good at painting actual "things". I mean something people would recognize. So, I figured I was not good at art.

And art was not something that was even just an acceptable hobby for anybody in my town. Manual labor was all that counted. Or if you were academically gifted you went off to college. It was one or the other. I don't remember anybody following an artistic path of any kind way back when. Or maybe just the one kid did, and he was the odd one out and talked about.

The grades I got in school for my essays were mediocre at best. I always got bored being told what to write about and pushed the instructions as far as I dared to write something a bit more interesting and fun. Also, "writer" is not even a job and writing can only ever be a hobby, right?

Fast forward to January 2021. After actually voicing my dream and letting the seed that was firmly planted start to grow, I actually got to a place where I knew I could do this. I was actively toying with the idea of writing a book for like 18 months but couldn't quite find the right angle. I knew it would have to do with mental health but how would I package it?

More time passed.

On April 2, 2024 I decided to just go for it. I had been writing on a regular basis and figured I'd just do it. No real plan up to that point. Nothing could have prepared me for what happened next. The mere thought of "Yes, I can!" made everything fall into place. I suddenly knew exactly how my book would be structured and that I would use my spring vacation to work on it.

That seed sure had started growing into something.

36 No quick fixes

THE JOURNEY – TIME TO RETHINK CORE BELIEFS

I'm not the most patient person. And those of you who know me personally have just laughed out loud. Understatement of the year, I know. Yet, I've had to be incredibly patient with myself these past four years. More so than I could have ever imagined.

You don't just take a list of wounds you'd like to heal and tick them off one by one and that's that. This is not a to-do list scenario. Each wound needs to be healed at the right time. Each wound needs time to heal at the right time. You can encourage the process, but you can't force it. Sitting here time and time again crying into a bucket of ice cream for no particular reason, unable to figure out why and where I was hurting was tough. It needed to happen though. And I needed to be okay with that.

And I needed people in my life who understood that this was part of the process. Who would just sit with me (virtually – this was still a pandemic world) and be emotionally mature enough to support me through it.

Every ice-cream-filled meltdown brought me closer to healing a part of me that was wounded. "Is the ice cream crucial?", I hear you ask. Well, it could be chocolate too, I guess; but yes, there needs to be some kind of soul food. I wouldn't have made it through otherwise. Healthy? Who cares?! I've been through a lot, and this is what I need.

I have since healed my relationship with food to a level where food doesn't scare me anymore and it doesn't occupy my mind 24/7. I'm an eating disorder survivor so this is a huge deal to me. A very liberating feeling.

But why does it all take so long? We are not good at marathons. Not many of us have actual marathon running experience. We try to take short cuts. We try to avoid change at all cost. We try to find a pill for whatever we want to change. We want that quick fix.

There are no quick fixes in trauma healing, and you're also never done. We all carry so many wounds within us that we could heal one wound every day for the rest of our lives. Smaller ones, bigger ones, medium-sized ones.

What we should do is heal the ones that affect our daily lives most and go from there. And once we start, more and more feelings that want to be dealt with will start appearing. Not all trauma is the big T kind. There are many smaller wounds that need healing too. And by smaller I don't mean less painful. I just mean that we don't perceive them as a big deal. Yet those can run deeper than bigger and more readily identified wounds.

And that's why trauma healing is a marathon and not a sprint. There are no quick fixes.

STEP IV: TIME TO HEAL

37 You used to be so much happier!

FEELINGS – TIME TO HEAL

People are telling me that I used to be so much happier. Well … People who knew me pre-2021 might say this to me. I was always smiling. I was always happy. Beaming smile on my face whenever I was around people. Do you know how exhausting that was? Do you know how much I was not true to myself?

Nobody is happy all the time and that's perfectly okay.

Today you know that if I smile, I actually mean it. It's no longer a mask. I no longer feel that I need to smile constantly for people to like me. Quite frankly, if the grumpy, sad or hurt version of me makes you uncomfortable, that's on you. I'm now team *don't ask me how I am if you don't want an honest answer*.

I don't mean that you should unload everything that's on your mind on unsuspecting bystanders. That's not what I'm saying. I just mean that it's okay not to be "fine" every single day – all day. I recently refused to answer that question for an entire day at work. My reply was "I'm not answering that question today, thank you". I got some weird looks, but it was the most self-compassionate answer I could give that day. What people made of it is none of my business.

Yes, even after you healed from your trauma there are triggers. You are not a machine. For me those triggers shifted from initiating a downward spiral that gripped me and was difficult to shake to something healthier. As an example, I will never be indifferent when it comes to child abuse. That's not going to happen. I will get angry at society, at the perpetrators, at anybody who still doesn't understand what abuse does to a child – it's 2024, get with it!

Today, I will speak up as it doesn't paralyze me anymore. I'm no longer trapped. I'm free to speak my mind. I needed to process all the emotions connected to my own trauma to get here. It took time.

I will also not stand by and listen to people calling suicide an easy way out or selfish. Once you've been there, you know that it's an entirely different story. Being empathic doesn't mean you haven't healed. It means that you are a human being with emotions. And one that is not afraid to show them and express them.

I will continue to call it "healing trauma", even though it's got more to do with processing emotions. Emotions you were not able to process or even feel when you were in survival mode. Or emotions you didn't know you needed to process when feelings get triggered and you realize there is underlying trauma.

Just like physical wounds leave scars – psychological wounds do as well. There will be moments those scars hurt and that's perfectly normal. It doesn't mean you haven't healed as much as you could. A scar is a scar.

Be gentle with yourself.

38 This is my responsibility? -That sucks!

UNDERSTANDING TRAUMA – TIME TO HEAL

Yes, it very much sucks that other people can cause immense trauma in us. Trauma that stays with us for decades. Trauma that causes auto-immune disorders. Trauma that causes mental health problems. Trauma that is unnecessary in the sense that it was completely man-made. Trauma that had one or several perpetrators.

And yes, it is up to us to "fix it". It is up to us to heal from it. I'm sitting here all grumpy because it's just so unfair. Yet, we are the only ones who can heal the trauma we've experienced. It's all stored in OUR body, OUR nervous system, OUR brain. We can get help accessing it. We can get help re-filing memories. We can get help processing emotions. Ultimately, it's up to us though.

That realization is a difficult one. Our sense of justice gets triggered in a major way. How is this fair?

Just how reluctant I am to being responsible for fixing other people's "mistakes" became apparent to me recently. I had gotten a letter that had not enough postage on it. Not usually a big deal as the sender gets notified and is asked to pay the missing amount. Then a couple of days later I received a *pay missing postage using this code* card. On it it said that the postal services had been unable to find the sender of the letter, and they were expecting me to pay the difference. Excuse me?!

 ➢ The sender didn't put enough postage on the letter – their responsibility.
 ➢ Swiss post delivered the letter anyway – their responsibility.
 ➢ They couldn't find the sender even though it was both on the front and the back of the envelope – their fault and responsibility.

I understand time pressure but finding people's addresses etc. is one of their core responsibilities. Come ON!

Yes, it was only 10 cents, and I could have easily paid it. Of course I could have. BUT every fiber of my being was like "nope, that's not going to happen". So instead, I chatted with a chatbot who clearly couldn't handle my passive aggressive "you know what I do when I try to find the sender of a letter? I check the envelope - front and back". It quickly said that I should probably talk to a real person. Well, duh!

It was resolved very quickly. They took full responsibility, and I didn't have to pay. It's all good.

I'm telling you this because I think it's an important example of what we are up against when starting the healing journey – defiance! The realization that it's our responsibility to figuratively pay those 10 cents every single time was a big one for me. An incredibly bitter pill to swallow.

It took me a long time to get from reading somewhere that it was up to me to heal my trauma and that nobody was coming to save me to actually understanding what that meant and getting over the "are you freaking kidding me – I'm NOT doing that as well!".

And then the healing began.

39 Linear my ass!

A lot of people operate under the misconception that healing from trauma is a linear process where you just increasingly get better. Well, how should I put this?

Nothing could be further from the truth. Once you start work there might be an overall upwards trajectory, but that doesn't mean that it can't go downhill really quickly at certain points in the process.

I think people need to be aware of this before they start because otherwise you have people who lose heart and give up when they are not feeling better every single day. It's such a dangerous misconception. Society as a whole really needs to do better here. It's crucial.

What held me back for a while was that I assumed that everybody else was always happy and because I wasn't and just pretended to be, I felt like a failure. I started working on healing my trauma but there was just so much - I felt overwhelmed.

It took a lot of effort and the right trigger to get to the bottom of a specific core trauma. When I did, it felt like hitting the jackpot. Puzzle pieces were falling into place. So many things were linked to it and got resolved as well. And then, the next big emotion got triggered and I explored that. I started from scratch but with previous experience under my belt. Starting to get the hang of it but not feeling better right at that moment.

Sometimes you need to go several rounds on one feeling or one memory and that's normal. It's not usually just a one off – it can happen but in my experience it rarely is. It feels a bit like a game of chutes and ladders. You can understand the game, know all the rules and still hit a chute once in a while. Or have the goal in sight and get knocked down again. Can we normalize that this is how healing trauma works?

Also, is there ever a time when you're fully healed? I'd say no to that. I'm very much a work in progress. But even if I had healed as much as I thought was possible, you never know where the next trigger might come from. Or you suddenly find out things you didn't know, and a new wound presents itself. This is when the healing work you have already done becomes a real asset. You start from experience and the process no longer scares you.

Even when everything is healed there are invisible scars and sometimes, they still hurt; just like a broken and now healed bone can hurt depending on the weather. And sometimes old feelings get triggered. Maybe it's time to reprocess them again or maybe it's a reminder of how far we've come.

It's never a measure of our success and it will never be a competition.

40 Feeling safe – with myself

SAFE? SAFE! – TIME TO HEAL

The most difficult part of getting out of survival mode was that I didn't always know that my reaction to certain situations had to do with survival mode and that it was an actual trauma response. Trusting my feelings felt kind of wrong. If my feelings were stuck in the past and holding me back, how was I ever gonna get anywhere?

Then step by step I started to realize that I could trust myself while paying attention to whether feelings were here and now feelings or rooted in the past. Slow progress that is still ongoing and will never end.

Feeling safe is such an important part of really feeling alive. Of feeling like you are in control. Of feeling like a human being that is enough the way they are.

You know when everybody tells you that feeling happy is what you should be striving for? Well, I'm gonna put "feeling safe" in the ring as the most important outcome of trauma healing. When you've lived in survival mode for decades, allowing your body and mind to feel safe is going to take a lot of practice and conscious effort. Your body and mind are not used to feeling safe. They are not used to not worrying. They are stuck in survival mode.

You are so used to living on high alert that when things are quiet you feel unsettled. You might even create chaos around you. You might deliberately look for danger. You might play with fire in different ways. You are not used to being safe. You are not used to being okay when things are peaceful, when they fall into place, when you are safe. That's why:

Safe feels boring. Safe feels wrong. You don't know how to feel safe.

You're used to feeling like the world is out to get you. Like everybody's conspired against you. Like bad things always happen when you start feeling good. When you dare to feel happy. When you are tentatively experiencing joy.

Waiting for that other shoe to drop. And then – if you wait long enough - there it is. All your fears are confirmed. You hide under the covers. You are just done with the world.

Then out of nowhere a friend reaches out. They hold your hand. They help you feel safe. Find that friend. Be that friend. Feeling safe is crucial for all of us.

Falling asleep holding that hand – pretending to hold that hand when they're not there. This sense of calm, this sense of *it's all going to be okay*. This sense of being able to let go of your pain and sorrow.

Just trust and friendship. There's safety in that. Hold on to it.

41 Women? – Too complicated!

SOCIETY SUCKS! - TIME TO HEAL

I'm a huge fan of science and science education. I went to the same high school Albert Einstein did after all. And yes, I mentioned it so anybody who had a pool going on this – you win.

Well, you don't really need ANY knowledge of science at all to realize that blood and saline solutions are two entirely different things. And as such they do behave differently too. I mean, where do I even start? Only now are period products tested with actual blood.

How? How is that even possible? How is a saline solution absorbed in the same way as blood? I don't want gross people out, but we're talking blood that comes with pieces of tissue as well. I don't even know what the thought process behind using a saline solution could have been. It's not science, it's common freaking sense.

And then there's the gaslighting that's been going on in terms of telling women about excellent absorption and how safe the products were and if we didn't agree it was clearly our fault. It's almost like society doesn't care about women. How easy would it be to test period products with blood?

And if THIS hasn't been done properly, what else are they hiding? This is super basic and super easy. Come on!

And here come the hormones. I'm well aware that men have hormones too, don't worry. Some of this might apply to men too, but, as I've said before, I can only talk about my own experience. And perimenopause is a bitch! There, I said it.

I started looking into how certain substances or over the counter drugs might influence hormone balance. You know what I noticed? There's not that much qualified information out there. And by qualified I mean proper scientific studies with many participants of all ages that are being tested during different stages of their menstrual cycles or who are in perimenopause. Doing that might actually yield useful information. You know what excuse is given? It's too complicated. We only test drugs on men or then on women who have gone through menopause. We can't have test and control groups that are all over the place – hormonally speaking.

Sure, let's exclude half the world's population from being given medication that is safe for them. Let's completely ignore the complexity of hormone-processes in our bodies. Let's pretend that if drugs have been tested on men, they are automatically safe for women of all ages. How is this practicing medicine? How is this scientific?

Hormones? Oh no, that's too complicated.

Next time I'm told "this excruciating pain is normal – all women go through this", I won't accept that as an answer. If ALL women are going through this, that must mean that scientists, doctors or whoever will have found a cure or something to help alleviate the symptoms, right? I mean that would be the logical conclusion. And don't get me started on women who've already gone through menopause and give you this knowing smile. The *suck it up, I went through that too* kind. It's exactly this attitude that won't bring change.

Rant over and I'm happy to be healing from societal norms and trauma. I'm very politely and calmly handing those norms back to society. I have no use for them any longer.

42 You can't meditate stress away - it's physics

STOP AND THINK! – TIME TO HEAL

How many people do you know that are stressed? How many of those people are trying to meditate or rest their stress away? I used to be one of them. Don't get me wrong, rest, sleep and meditation are useful and sleep is especially necessary. You can't survive without it.

But is it the antidote to stress? I have an absolutely unscientific theory on that.

Let's start by defining the equilibrium we are seeking. You know that state in which we feel relaxed and balanced. If we put that in the middle and think about what's at opposite ends of that scale. Let's put stress at one end and maybe fun at the other. In order for that scale to be balanced there need to be equal amounts of fun to counterweight the stress. I hope you're with me so far.

If we look at this in terms of physics and assume your stress level is high, the scale is completely out of balance. The stress is weighing you down. Picture it. The stress side is all the way down. Then there's the equilibrium we're seeking in the middle. How are 24 hours of meditation, extra sleep, trying to relax going to change anything? You can't bring the stress level back to a balanced state by piling onto the middle of the scale. Nothing is going to move. Nothing is going to change. The stress won't decrease when you realize your meditation doesn't work and more sleep doesn't help either. It will stay high.

So, to counterbalance the stress, do something fun. Something that puts you in a state of flow. You need to go to the opposite end of the spectrum. I called it "fun" because it seemed closest to the opposite of stressful/stressed - especially since "relaxed" is taken for the balanced state we're striving for. And to me "fun" is anything that you enjoy doing.

Now, before you say "but I enjoy meditating" remember that I wrote this for people who don't find meditation helpful. I wrote this for people who relate to physics better than to the practice of meditation. And I wrote it for people who are tired of others telling them to try and relax and meditate when they are stressed.

On that note, movement helps. How about yoga or tai chi as a fun way to meditate? Or I started painting. Not a lot of movement, but the fun kind. Now when you think "fun" what comes to mind? And how many hours a day do you spend doing that fun thing?

I don't have scientific studies to quote. Just my brain trying to make sense of why rest and sleep didn't help me when I was stressed. Realizing that in physics a scale with stress weighing heavily on one side wouldn't move the tiniest bit if you just piled on the middle. That's where the calm and relaxed state is. That's where we'd like to get to. It's a state, not an action.

Once I started looking at the physics of it and deliberately added fun sequences to my day, things started looking up.

Another thing I started doing was ignoring people who said I should try meditation or rest and sleep more. I now just assume they don't know their physics.

43 I'm enough!

WHO CARES? – TIME TO HEAL

Time to look at healing and getting to a feeling of being enough – just the way we are. To get there we need to look at managing expectations. Let's start with social media, because why not?

We post something. We leave. We come back. We see comments and likes. What happens next has a lot to do with our expectations. If we have no expectations, any *like* will be a positive, any comment a (hopefully positive) surprise; negative comments don't hurt as much because we didn't expect positive ones.

Now, if we expect people to really like what we posted, *likes* are not seen as positive, since we were expecting those; we were also expecting positive comments – those are just ticked off as well. Negative comments however – those really hurt, because they don't match our expectations. Be careful out there!

Then there are societal expectations. Those we can't control, but we can realize it's happening and speak up. Here's some of what society told me I was guilty of so far:

> - I'm not a boy – how fucking dare I!
> - I don't fit into a neurotypical framework – how scary!
> - I'm excellent at math – "but you're a girl!"
> - I don't wear make-up and don't own any high-heeled shoes – "but you're a girl!"
> - I never went through a party phase - I'd much rather read a book.
> - I've never tried drugs – my brain is crazy enough as is.
> - I've never been drunk – such a freak!
> - I'm a fat hiker – sue me!

Most of this is still going on today. I have spoken up in the past and you will find societal rants in this book too. All this is telling people they are not enough. This is so harmful. Just let people be who they are. Think of how much money (in therapy) could be saved if people were taught that they are **OKAY** just the way they are!

You are all enough!

There you go, now that we realize that we can start healing. It's harder than it sounds. Those core beliefs and expectations run super deep. We start by recognizing things, patterns, expectations that we internalized and that are not actually our own. We start looking at what we really want, feel or like.

I had to go back to early childhood to re-discover some of the things I am now passionate about. I keep discovering more and more things that I stopped doing for whatever reason. It could be anything. Your dialect, the way you dress, your hobbies, your haircut. Go as crazy as you can with what you truly want and who you truly are. You deserve it. Worry about yourself and let others think whatever they want.

As for anything about yourself that you can't change. Take good care of that too – especially of the complicated feelings attached to it. Acceptance starts within ourselves. And trust me I know how hard this is. I'm still struggling as I write this.

Remember that you can't change who you are and why would anybody want to change the wonderful person you are anyway?

Healing starts with self-acceptance. You got this!

44 It's everywhere! Calling it out!

GASLIGHTING – TIME TO HEAL

It's been a long road from actively paying attention to gaslighting, to understanding how it works, to rethinking core beliefs, to actually using my voice to heal from all that and calling it out.

Calling it out when it comes to body weight. You can't go around telling people how to lose weight every five minutes and that it's all their fault and that they are unhealthy and unworthy and when they are feeling bad about themselves you turn around and tell those very same people to love themselves just the way they are. Do you see how insane that is?

Calling it out when I hear people's experiences being negated. Nope, we are not too sensitive, you're just not ready to hear how your actions are making other people feel. That is a you problem. If somebody tells you how a certain situation is making them feel, that's how it's making them feel. Period. It doesn't matter if what you said was a joke and they should have known. It doesn't matter if you can understand how they are feeling. It is how they are feeling. If you can't see that as the starting point to the resolution of any issues, you'll fail.

And I've written that last paragraph also for all of us. We tend to gaslight ourselves into thinking our feelings are somehow wrong or how we experience things doesn't matter. But we've established that our body doesn't forget. Our nervous system is trying to give us signals. Let's not ignore them.

Listen when people are talking about their experiences. It helps you understand. And if your answer to women speaking up about abuse is "not all men" instead of calling out the bad behavior we are talking about, well, what can I say … It means that you know this behavior is happening because you have firsthand experience of it (seeing it or participating in it) and you think because not every single man on this planet is doing it, it somehow doesn't matter. And that makes sense to you?

Writing about this and calling it out whenever/wherever I can has helped me heal from the gaslighting I experienced myself. It's all over the place and it's part of most people's lives without them even realizing it. Healing for me is knowing about it and getting better and better at calling it out.

It makes me feel like I have a voice and like I have agency. Like I can do something about it. Of course I'm not able to solve this on my own, but pointing out instances of gaslighting and introducing that concept to people has been a pretty successful endeavor. Putting a spotlight on gaslighting to take its power away and for people to recognize it and be able to stand up against it is a good first step.

We're all in this together.

45 Boundaries? Yes, please

FORGIVENESS – TIME TO HEAL

Setting boundaries. What a concept! And so freaking difficult to do. I mean I had stepped over my own boundaries on several occasions. I set them and let people cross them without consequences. Step one was forgiving myself for letting people treat me like that. That's a tough start. I mean it was my responsibility to walk away when those boundaries were crossed, and I somehow couldn't.

A lot of self-blame went into that. Something I needed to understand.

Boundaries are really just another word for consequences. We're not trying to change somebody else's behavior. We are just communicating what we're willing to accept and where we draw the line. If we constantly get made fun of or talked down to at gatherings one such boundary could be "if you insist on talking to me like this, I won't be coming to future events". And that's that. They can continue their behavior; you just won't be there to witness or be a target of it.

I'm sure you've seen those memes around that say stuff like "the only people who will have a problem with your boundaries are the ones who were benefiting from your lack of them". Setting boundaries and protecting yourself will annoy people, but only people you are better off without anyway.

Others will accept your boundaries and act accordingly. Boundaries can never come between friends or destroy healthy relationships. Then again, those people are also the people who make a mistake, apologize for it, change their behavior and make sure it doesn't happen again. No forgiveness needed. In this case it'll go something like "yikes, I'm so sorry that was totally my fault. I really screwed up" – "Yes, you did. And thank you for acknowledging that."

Do you see how much healthier that is? Healthier than "it's okay" – which it really isn't. Let's normalize thanking people for apologies and not invalidating our own feelings of hurt in the process. It is not okay that they did something to hurt us. Period.

I was talking boundaries, so let's get back to those. I needed to learn that a boundary was not me telling somebody how I want them to act towards me. That's not it at all. It's much more powerful than that.

You can tell somebody that you don't want them to talk to you in a certain way. We've already established that if they talk down to you, they don't respect you. Why do you think they will change their behavior in any way if you ask them nicely? That's never going to happen.

There needs to be a consequence, aka a boundary. So instead we say "if you talk down to me, I will walk away". The difficult part is to actually do it. A steep learning curve on that one too.

Of course, if the person you're dealing with has narcissistic tendencies or is emotionally immature, they will play the victim in this case and tell everybody that you no longer talk to them or that you walked away and that they have no idea why. But this shouldn't surprise you at this point. Time to cut some ties.

Healthy boundaries beat forgiveness hands down. It's not even a contest and if it was one, not a close one at all. Boundaries for the win.

46 A matter of perspective

HEALING TRAUMA – TIME TO HEAL

We all have stories from our childhood that we never questioned. I certainly have many. At some point I started looking at them more closely and there were so many inconsistencies. Some of it just didn't make sense. I totally get that adults sometimes tell little white lies or keep things from children to protect them. I'd consider that pretty normal.

But what about traumatic events that are stuck in our body and that influence us to this day? Are those stories really true the way we remember them? Are they still affecting us because we haven't moved out of the kid perspective?

I have some childhood trauma where I felt super helpless. I couldn't help me myself (aged four); I was completely out of my depth and understandably so. There were no other adults around to help me either. Or they were on board with what was happening and not speaking up. Which in turn made me think the situation that presented itself to me was normal. Vicious cycle that.

As adults we come to understand that we can always do something. We have agency. Sometimes it is not possible to change a situation but maybe we can change our role in it or maybe we can even walk away. We don't have to be stuck. Being stuck is our "I'm helpless" trauma response talking. We can always do something. No matter how small the action, agency gives us power.

I found this realization very healing. I don't need to be stuck in my trauma response; I can change things around. I can change my perspective. As ever it is crucial that I acknowledge that feeling of helplessness and in my case also acknowledge that four-year-old me really was helpless in that situation. So, step one was to stop being annoyed at myself for not speaking up when I was four years old.

This sounds obvious to you? Good. In that case I'm just gonna whisper that "you have such self-blame events too" and leave it at that.

97

Another important situation where healing was a matter of perspective for me was when I started talking about things that happened and realized that my normal was not "normal". Initially that blew my mind. I mean my life was all I knew. Yes, I saw that other families were different. I mean all families were different in their own special way as far as I was concerned. No surprise there.

It felt good to talk about what I was struggling with and have people in my life who understood, who listened without judgment and offered their outside perspective. Being understood or getting the sense that people are trying to understand, has proved absolutely invaluable.

Even just that fact has healed wounds, and I shouldn't say "just" here. Acknowledging how others are feeling and trying to understand what brought them to that point, then offering your own perspective where appropriate, you might just help somebody turn their life around because they finally feel heard and understood.

47 I'm a writer!

I started writing on a regular basis in the fall of 2023. I created a series called "Sunday Morning Thoughts". This just happened. It wasn't planned at all. What it gave me was focus and a reason for writing every Sunday morning. And you know what? Being able to stick with it and just put random thoughts out there every Sunday had a healing effect like you would not believe.

It was never about people's reactions – although they have been mostly positive. I was and am writing for myself. I have found my voice and I plan on using it every step of the way. Especially writing about mental health struggles and how I was able to overcome them. Wow, how powerful. Putting things into words and trying to help people understand what might be going on with their own mental health or how to support a loved one, has had such a profound effect on me.

If even just one person finds something I write helpful, it's well worth the effort.

I was very young when I felt like I wanted to write. I mean I read a lot and it seemed to make sense. It was the *how* that was blocking me and the having to find a real job attitude of my environment. I don't think I actually dared ever even voice this dream.

Turns out I first needed to become proficient in English and be asked by a friend I hadn't yet met in person and who lived across an ocean what my dream was for me to remember. So that gut feeling I had as a child was right, I needed to become a writer. It was my subconscious telling me how I would be able to heal.

How did it help me heal?

I had to try to make sense of what was going on in my mind – very healing. If I could explain what was happening to a friend or my newsletter readers, then surely it would start making sense to me as well.

It's the old *if you can explain it to somebody, you've truly understood it*. My mind needed a focus. Mental health and overcoming trauma was that focus. The interesting thing is that it didn't really seem to matter what I was writing about initially. I just needed to get started. Thinking things through while walking and then writing them down was the perfect way for me to do just that.

Today I can proudly say that I AM a writer and that writing has helped me heal.

48 Making the scars look pretty – pretty amazing that is

THE JOURNEY – TIME TO HEAL

This chapter was supposed to be called something like "thriving" or "living my best life". Okay, I'll admit that it was never going to be called the latter. That's just not me. And I wish I could call this chapter "thriving" because I've made such incredible progress. I am immensely proud of what I achieved and how I reinvented myself. So much so.

But "thriving"? Well, in a way yes. Compared to where I was four years ago. Most definitely. Still, the healing process is ongoing. A lot more things to untangle. And I'm sure many more core beliefs to rethink and abandon for healthier ones.

What I will say though is that I have managed to make my scars look prettier than they would have done without me giving painting a try. That was such an important part of healing. Just letting the creative juices flow. Switching off my brain like that was initially very scary. I didn't know how to switch off my brain. And I still don't think you can. At least not really.

And why would you?

What I managed to do was to not think about what I wanted to paint. That's why I'm going to stick to abstract painting. I get painter's block whenever I start trying to create something specific. Is painter's block even a thing? No idea, but it feels like the best way I know how to express what happens.

I mentioned scars left on our nervous system, on our brain, on our souls - if that's a concept we accept. Trauma leaves scars behind all over the place. It's part of life. I have managed to identify and heal so many injuries I never even knew were there. They were the underlying ones; hidden behind bigger wounds that I was already aware of. It's such an incredibly complicated and powerful process and I've mastered that.

Having mastered it doesn't mean that there is no more work to do, it just means that I am very confident I now have the tools to deal with anything.

And while I live my life in the knowledge that there is more trauma out there for me to process, I might as well paint my emotions onto canvas and maybe – just maybe, some of that art speaks to people.

It sure has helped me release emotions and make them look pretty - pretty amazing. I'm in a good place. I know more work lies ahead but looking back and seeing how far I've come, I'm proud. And I say – bring it on universe, bring it on.

I've learned that I can handle anything that's thrown at me, even – and especially if – it's from within. The universe has nothing I can't handle, I have to watch out for what my nervous system and my soon to be retired kid brain bring up. They have done their very best to protect me early on in life. Now, I have to let them relax and trust that I will do my best and be able to keep myself safe.

That was my biggest lesson throughout this journey. Releasing the kid brain and trusting myself.

I got this!

49 Hope

I was reminded of why I started writing the other day. Whatever your trauma, whatever your struggle, I'm writing to give you hope. If I can make it from the brink of suicide to where I am now, there must be hope for everybody out there. And ... I used to absolutely hate when people said that. Mainly because I was feeling hopeless and stuck.

So, that's the task for today - believing there is hope. That's all I did when a seed of hope was planted in January 2020. I started thinking about the possibility of hope. The possibility of change. Not in a big way, just in a positive "what if" kind of way.

My brain did the rest. It was a slow process, and I did need encouragement along the way. It was nowhere near straight progress. I couldn't even see the proverbial light at the end of the tunnel yet. I was pretty much still stuck way deep in that tunnel.

But now I had a flashlight with me and was trying to find my way. I was not walking on a smooth surface, so I stubbed my toes and fell on several occasions. Walking back the wrong way until I realized things were getting darker again. I held on to that flashlight tightly. I wasn't going to give up my little ray of hope.

The more I started talking about things (my life, my struggles etc.) the more people I could feel walking with me or shining a light for me. Some of them were like lighthouses guiding me from afar – people I was yet to meet. It took me a good nine months to get even close to the end of the tunnel. And this was after decades of being stuck in there without a light. In there where it was safe. In there where I could hide.

And I tell you what, this is when it got really scary. This is when I would have backed out if it wasn't for certain friends. This was when I was the most worried that I couldn't do it. I was so close to the exit, and I was shaking like a leaf. I dropped my flashlight. Luckily, I no longer needed it.

Very unexpectedly a group of new friends was waiting right there to greet me and welcomed me to my new life with open arms.

For now, I just want you to know you're not alone. That there is hope. There are people with flashlights. There are big old lighthouses – even in landlocked Switzerland.

We're all in this together.

Inspiration

Acknowledging friends

There are so many people I want to thank, but I like to do things differently. Basically, if you've been a positive part of my life the past four years – I appreciate you. I have friends whose names range from A to Z, and also in AZ. And it just happens that some As and a Z deserve special thanks, but then there's also a couple of awesome Ds and a very special W. And really everybody else from It's Just Us. Love you guys!

X might be the only letter I can't come up with a name or place for off the top of my head, but if we go with X-Twitter then I can safely say that I met most of my new friends thanks to social media.

So, there's that.

Some of these friends have inspired and supported me throughout this entire process and I think I have been pretty good about letting them know how much that means/meant to me. But I can't write a book without singling out David Ippolito aka That Guitar Man from Central Park. I really can't. I tried. He, as the wonderful human being he is, and through his music, inspired me beyond belief.

Acknowledging inspiring resources

I didn't follow a given path or follow any people in particular, but I need to mention Brené Brown. Her TED Talk on shame did something to me. It planted a seed of sorts. Then I started reading books like *Girl, stop apologizing* by Rachel Hollins or *Brave, Not Perfect* by Reshma Saujani. By that time, I was way on my way to start paying attention.

Somehow, I found Mel Robbins and listened to a bunch of her podcasts – I find her very relatable. She also talked about dreams. Something stuck from there. I still think she is brilliant. I also think I found Steven Bartlett and his podcast through her. Difficult to remember that chain.

While I was moving more towards trauma and trauma healing – it might have even been something Mel said that brought me there – I found Dr. Julie Smith. Her explanations of psychological processes in her book *Why has nobody told me this before* and also – or especially - her short videos made it feel like mental health struggles were something one could overcome.

Now I could add a list of sources to the back of this book. They would range from Gabor Maté to Bessel van der Kolk possibly passing Francine Shapiro. And while I have books by all those authors on my bookshelf, I have to say that I only read selected passages in them and that was that. And you can easily find all those books on trauma and trauma healing on your own.

Sometimes I wish I'd gotten to know about some of their work earlier in my journey. Then again, I managed to figure all this out by myself too. It might have taken a bit longer, but it stuck because it is MY experience and not something I read somewhere.

What I wanted to mention here was one book that was a bit of a game changer in its simplicity and powerful messages. It's *The Boy, the Mole, the Fox and the Horse* by Charlie Mackesy. Read that before you do anything else. I have three quotes from that book written on the wall in my bedroom.

Powerful. Inspiring. It will make you cry. It will give you hope.

About the author

A creative powerhouse who speaks her mind. A trauma survivor with too many adverse childhood experiences to count who has fought her way back into life in her mid to late forties.

Born and raised in Switzerland, I studied English Language and Literature at the University of Zurich (M.A.), followed that up with a BSc in Psychology and a degree in Secondary Education.

I worked in many different fields including banking (IT), marketing, education, teaching.

I only recently started writing and following my creative side. I also love hiking all over Switzerland. And languages or language as such give me great pleasure. Switzerland is a great place to live for most of those endeavors.

About the picture: it was taken close to my 49th birthday in the Netherlands. My hair got tangled up and untangling that almost matched untangling my entire life in terms of complexity and pain.